Alexis

CCSS/PARCC Prep
Grade 4
Reading Comprehension

by E.J. von Schoff

Student Book ISBN: 978-1-4973-9796-5 • Class Pack ISBN: 978-0-7827-2327-4
Item Code RAS 2727 • Copyright © 2014 Queue, Inc.

Queue, Inc. • 80 Hathaway Drive, Stratford, CT 06615
(800) 232-2224 • Fax: (800) 775-2729 • www.qworkbooks.com

Table of Contents

A LETTER FROM THE PRESIDENT TO HIS DAUGHTER

by Theodore Roosevelt

Keystone Ranch, Jan. 29, 1901

Darling Little Ethel,

1   You would be much amused with the animals round the ranch. The most thoroughly independent and self-possessed of them is a large white pig, which we have <u>christened</u> "Maude." She goes everywhere at her own will; she picks up scraps from the dogs, who <u>bay</u> dismally at her, but know they have no right to kill her; and then she eats the green alfalfa hay from the two milk cows who live in the big corral with the horses.

2   One of the dogs has just had a litter of puppies; you would love them, with their little wrinkled noses and squeaky voices.

1   Where was President Roosevelt when he wrote this letter?

A   At home
B   On a ranch
C   At the White House
D   On a boat

2 In paragraph 1, *christened* means —

A   invited
B   named
C   recognized
D   watched

3   Look at these definitions of the word *bay*.

> 1. Bark
> 2. Cove
> 3. Harbor
> 4. Parking area

Which one explains the meaning of *bay* in paragraph 1?

A   Definition 1
B   Definition 2
C   Definition 3
D   Definition 4

4   This letter is about —

A   puppies
B   barking dogs
C   what cows eat
D   animals on a ranch

THE LITTLE BUSY BEE

by Isaac Watts

1   How doth the little busy bee
        Improve each shining <u>hour</u>,
        And gather honey all the day
        From every opening <u>flower</u>!

2   How skillfully she builds her cell!
        How neat she spreads the wax!
        And labors hard to store it well
        With the <u>sweet food</u> she makes.

3   In works of labor or of skill
        I would be busy too:
        For Satan finds some mischief still
        For idle hands to do.

4   In books, or work, or healthful play
        Let my first years be passed,
        That I may give for every day
        Some good account at last.

1   The speaker in this poem —

    A is afraid of bees
    B likes eating honey
    C watches bees all day
    D admires bees for all they do

2   What is the "sweet food" mentioned in verse 2?

    A Flowers
    B Honey
    C Nectar
    D Wax

3   How does the speaker want to keep busy?

    A   Keeping bees and making honey
    B   Reading, working, and exercising
    C   Keeping bees
    D   Gardening

4   Why does the speaker want to keep busy?

    A   He is bored with watching the bee.
    B   People who do nothing might get punished.
    C   He wants to be active in order to stay healthy.
    D   People with nothing to do may get into trouble.

5   Look at the words hour and flower in the first verse of the poem. These words are a good example of —

    A   free verse
    B   meter
    C   rhyme
    D   rhythm

4

TWO FABLES

THE PENNY-WISE MONKEY

1   Once upon a time, the king of a large, rich country gathered together his army to attack a small, faraway country. The king and his soldiers marched all morning long and then made camp in the forest.

2   When the soldiers fed the horses, they gave them some peas to eat. One of the monkeys living in the forest saw the peas and jumped down to get some of them. He filled his mouth and hands with them. Then, he went up into the tree again and sat down to eat the peas.

3   As he sat there eating the peas, one pea fell from his hand to the ground. At once, the greedy monkey dropped all the peas he had in his hands and ran down to hunt for the lost pea. But he could not find it. He climbed up into his tree again and sat still, looking very glum. "To get more, I threw away what I had," he said to himself.

4   The king watched the monkey. Afterwards, he said to himself: "I will not be like that foolish monkey, who lost much to gain so little. I will go back to my own country and enjoy what I already have."

5   Then he and his men marched back home.

THE DOG AND HIS REFLECTION

1   A dog, to whom a butcher had thrown a bone, was hurrying home with his prize as fast as he could go. As he crossed a narrow footbridge, he happened to look down and see himself reflected in the quiet water as if in a mirror. But the greedy dog thought he was looking at a real dog carrying a bone much bigger than his own.

2   If he had stopped to think, he would have known better.

3   But instead of thinking, he dropped his bone and sprang at the dog in the river, only to find himself swimming for dear life to reach the shore. At last, he managed to scramble out, and as he stood sadly thinking about the good bone he had lost, he realized what a stupid dog he had been.

5

1   In the first fable, why is the army on the march?

    A   To go hunting
    B   To take over another country
    C   To harvest peas to feed its horses
    D   To protect the king from his enemies

2   In the second fable, what does the dog see in the water?

    A   Another dog carrying a bone
    B   Himself carrying his own bone
    C   A dog swimming toward him to take his bone
    D   A bone that is much bigger than his own floating by

3   In the first fable, why does the king decide not to attack the small country?

    A   He does not want to risk losing what he already has.
    B   The country is so small that it is not worth fighting for.
    C   He feels sorry for the monkey who has lost all his peas.
    D   There are no more peas to feed his army's horses.

4   How are the monkey and the dog alike?

    A   Neither has anything to eat.
    B   Both steal food from other animals.
    C   Both throw away what they have to get more.
    D   Each thinks his reflection is another animal with food.

5   Both fables warn the reader against

    A   greed
    B   hunger
    C   stealing
    D   thinking

WEBPAGE: STUFFED CELERY STICKS

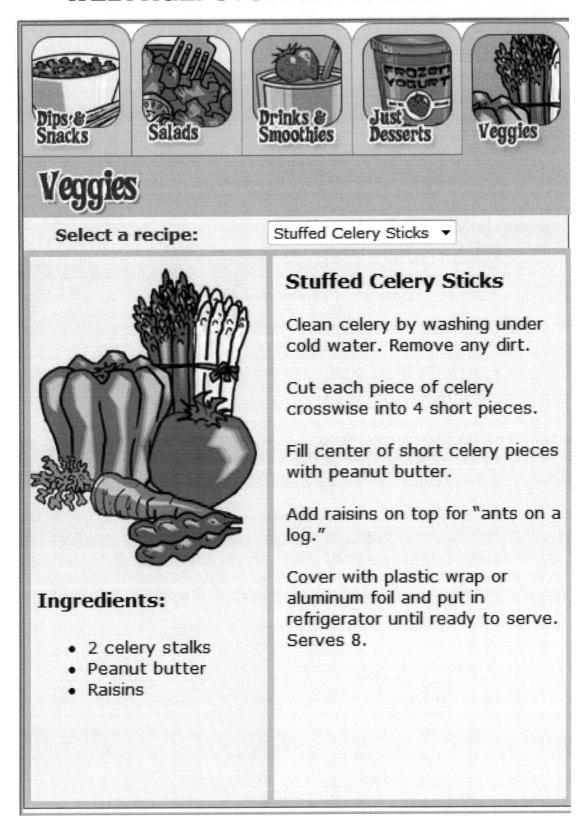

Dips & Snacks   **Salads**   **Drinks & Smoothies**   **Just Desserts**   **Veggies**

Veggies

Select a recipe: [Stuffed Celery Sticks ▼]

Stuffed Celery Sticks

Clean celery by washing under cold water. Remove any dirt.

Cut each piece of celery crosswise into 4 short pieces.

Fill center of short celery pieces with peanut butter.

Add raisins on top for "ants on a log."

Cover with plastic wrap or aluminum foil and put in refrigerator until ready to serve. Serves 8.

Ingredients:

- 2 celery stalks
- Peanut butter
- Raisins

Source: BAM! Body and Mind, Centers for Disease Control and Prevention (www.bam.gov).

7

1   To find a recipe for potato salad, which tab would you click?

    A   Dips and Snacks
    B   Salads
    C   Drinks and Smoothies
    D   Just Desserts

2   To make this recipe, you would stuff the celery with —

    A   cream cheese
    B   peanut butter
    C   chocolate
    D   yogurt

3   What is the first step in making this recipe?

    A   adding the raisins
    B   cutting the celery
    C   filling the celery
    D   washing the celery

4   How many pieces of stuffed celery are in a serving?

    A   One
    B   Two
    C   Four
    D   Eight

5   This text —

    A   compares different ways to prepare celery
    B   lists the steps in making stuffed celery
    C   explains reasons for eating celery
    D   gives examples of types of celery

WHY MR. SNAKE CANNOT WINK

by Thornton W. Burgess

1 Peter Rabbit and Johnny Chuck were playing tag on the Green Meadows. It happened that curled up on a little grassy tussock, taking an early morning sun-bath, lay little Mr. Greensnake. Of course, Peter Rabbit and Johnny Chuck were not afraid of him. If it had been Mr. Rattlesnake or Mr. Gophersnake, it would have been different. But from little Mr. Greensnake there was nothing to fear, and sometimes, just for fun, Peter would jump right over him. When he did that, Peter always winked good-naturedly. But Mr. Greensnake never winked back. Instead, he would raise his head, run his tongue out at Peter, and hiss in what he tried to make a very fierce and angry manner. Then Peter would laugh and wink at him again. But never once did Mr. Greensnake wink back.

2 Peter was thinking of this as he and Johnny Chuck stretched out in a sunny spot to get their breath and rest. He had never thought of it before, but now that he had noticed it, he couldn't remember that he ever had seen little Mr. Greensnake wink—nor any of Mr. Greensnake's relatives. He mentioned the matter to Johnny Chuck.

3 "That's so," replied Johnny thoughtfully. "I've never seen any of them wink, either. Do you suppose they can wink?"

4 "Let's go ask Mr. Greensnake," said Peter.

5 Up they hopped and raced over to the grassy tussock where Mr. Greensnake lay, but to all their questions he would make no reply save to run out his tongue at them. Finally, they gave up asking him.

6 "I tell you what. Let's go over to the Smiling Pool and ask Grandfather Frog. He'll be sure to know, and perhaps, if he is feeling good, he'll tell us a story," said Peter.

7 So off they scampered to the Smiling Pool. There they found Grandfather Frog sitting on his big green lily-pad just as usual, and Peter knew by the look in his great, goggly eyes that Grandfather Frog had a good breakfast of foolish green flies tucked away inside his white and yellow waistcoat. His eyes twinkled as Peter and Johnny very politely wished him good morning. "Good morning," said Grandfather Frog gruffly.

8 But Peter had seen that twinkle in his eyes and knew that Grandfather Frog was feeling good-natured in spite of his <u>gruff</u> greeting.

9   "If you please, Grandfather Frog, why doesn't Mr. Greensnake wink at us when we wink at him?" he asked.

10   "Chug-a-rum! Because he can't," replied Grandfather Frog.

11   "Can't!" cried Peter Rabbit and Johnny Chuck together.

12   "That's what I said—can't," replied Grandfather Frog. "And no more can Mr. Blacksnake, or Mr. Rattlesnake, or Mr. Gophersnake, or any other member of the Snake family."

13   "Why not?" cried Peter and Johnny, all in the same breath.

14   "Chug-a-rum!" said Grandfather Frog, folding his hands across his white and yellow waistcoat, "if you will sit still until I finish, I'll tell you; but if you move or ask any foolish questions, I'll stop right where I am, and you'll never hear the end of the story, for no one else knows it."

15   Of course, Peter and Johnny promised to sit perfectly still and not say a word. After they had made themselves comfortable, Grandfather Frog cleared his throat as if to begin, but for a long time, he didn't say a word. Once Peter opened his mouth to ask why, but remembered in time and closed it again without making a sound.

16   At last, Grandfather Frog cleared his throat once more, and, with a far-away look in his great, goggly eyes, began: "Once upon a time, long, long ago, when the world was young, lived old Mr. Snake, the grandfather a thousand times removed of little Mr. Greensnake and all the other Snakes whom you know. Of course, he wasn't old then. He was young and spry and smart, was Mr. Snake. Now, there is such a thing as being too smart. That was the trouble with Mr. Snake. Yes, Sir, that was the trouble with Mr. Snake. He was so smart that he soon found out that he was the smartest of all the meadow and forest people, and that was a bad thing. It certainly was a very bad thing."

17   Grandfather Frog shook his head gravely. "You see," he continued, "as soon as he found that out, he began to take advantage of his neighbors and cheat them, but he would do it so smoothly that they never once suspected that they were being cheated. Mr. Snake would go about all day cheating everybody he met. At night, he would go home and chuckle over his smartness. It wasn't long before he began to look down on his neighbors for being so honest that they didn't suspect other people of being dishonest and for being so easily cheated.

18   "Now, one bad habit almost always leads to another. From cheating, Mr. Snake just naturally slipped to stealing. Yes, Sir, he became a thief. Of course, that made trouble right away, but still no one suspected Mr. Snake. He was always very polite to everyone and always offering to do favors for his neighbors. In fact, Mr. Snake was very well liked and much respected. When any one had been robbed, he was always the first to offer sympathy and join in the hunt for the thief. He was so spry and slim, and could slip through the tall grass so fast, that he could go almost where he pleased without being seen, and this made him very bold. If he did happen to be found near the scene of trouble, he always had a story ready to account for his presence, and it sounded so true, and he told it in such an honest manner, that no one thought of doubting it.

19   "So Mr. Snake found that lying helped him to cheat and steal, and all the time he kept thinking how smart he was. But even Mr. Snake had a little bit of conscience, and once in a while it would trouble him. So what do you think he did? Why, cheating had become such a habit with him that he actually tried to cheat himself—to cheat his conscience! When he was telling a lie, he would wink one eye. 'That,' said he to himself, 'means that it isn't true, and if these folks are not smart enough to see me wink and know what it means, it's their own fault if they believe what I'm telling them.' But always he took care to wink the eye that was turned away from the one he was talking to.

20   "Dear me, dear me, such terrible times as there were on the Green Meadows and in the Green Forest! They grew worse and worse, and when at last Old Mother Nature came to see how all the little people were getting along, she heard so many complaints that she hardly knew where to begin to straighten matters out. She had all the little people come before her in turn and tell their troubles. When it came Mr. Snake's turn, he had no complaint to make. He seemed to be the only one who had no troubles. She asked him a great many questions, and for each one he had a ready reply. Of course, a great many of these replies were lies, and every time he told one of these, he winked without knowing it. You see, it had become a habit.

21   "Now, with all his smartness, Mr. Snake had forgotten one thing—one very important thing. It was this: You can't fool Old Mother Nature, and it is of no use to try. He hadn't been talking three minutes before she knew who was at the bottom of all the trouble. She let him finish, then called all the others about her and told them who had made all the trouble. Mr. Snake was very bold. He held his head very high in the air and pretended not to care. When Old Mother Nature turned her head, he even ran out his tongue at her, just as all the Snake family do at you and me today. When she had finished telling them how cheating and stealing and lying isn't smart at all, but very, very dreadful, she turned to Mr. Snake and said, 'From this time on, no one will

11

believe anything you say, and you shall have no friends. You will never wink again, for you and your children and your children's children forever will have no eyelids, so all the world may know that people who misuse the things given them shall have them taken away.'

22 "And now you know why little Mr. Greensnake cannot wink at you—he hasn't any eyelids to wink with," finished Grandfather Frog.

23 Peter Rabbit drew a long breath. "Thank you, oh, thank you ever so much, Grandfather Frog," he said. "Will you tell us next time why Bobby Coon wears rings on his tail?"

24 "Perhaps," replied Grandfather Frog.

1 Peter winks at Mr. Greensnake and wonders —

    A if the snake will hurt him
    B why snakes never wink back
    C why snakes lie out in the sun
    D why snakes run out their tongues

2 Peter and Johnny hope that Grandfather Frog —

    A will tell them a story
    B knows why snakes wink
    C is feeling good-natured today
    D knows why snakes run out their tongues

3 In paragraph 8, what does *gruff* mean?

    A Good-natured
    B Grumpy
    C Hoarse
    D Friendly

4   Which of these words best describes Grandfather Frog?

   A   active
   B   dishonest
   C   unfriendly
   D   wise

5   In Grandfather Frog's story, when did Mr. Snake wink?

   A   When he said hello
   B   Whenever he told a joke
   C   Whenever he told a lie
   D   When he felt tired

6   What do you think Peter and Johnny learned from Grandfather Frog's story?

   A   Never to wink at snakes
   B   Not to cheat, steal, and lie
   C   Never to fool Mother Nature
   D   Not to talk to Grandfather Frog

7. What got Mr Snake in trouble in the first place, according to the story?

   A   He had no conscience
   B   You can't fool Mother Nature
   C   He was too smart
   D   He was so spry and slim, and could slip through the tall grass so fast, that
       he could go almost where he pleased without being seen, and this made
       him very bold.

7A Which of the following passages supports the answer you provided to the question above?

A He was so smart that he soon found out that he was the smartest of all the meadow and forest people, and that was a bad thing. It certainly was a very bad thing.

B It wasn't long before he began to look down on his neighbors for being so honest that they didn't suspect other people of being dishonest and for being so easily cheated.

C He was always very polite to everyone and always offering to do favors for his neighbors. In fact, Mr. Snake was very well liked and much respected. When any one had been robbed, he was always the first to offer sympathy and join in the hunt for the thief.

D If he did happen to be found near the scene of trouble, he always had a story ready to account for his presence, and it sounded so true, and he told it in such an honest manner, that no one thought of doubting it.

8. How did an unusual kind of cheating lead to Mr. Snake's punishment?

_____

_____

_____

_____

_____

_____

_____

_____

_____

_____

PILGRIM CHILDREN

1   In New England in the 1600s, children had to work hard. They had many chores. They had to fetch water from the brook or spring, gather firewood, and herd animals. Children spent time gathering berries and other wild plants. They also helped their parents to cook, clean, preserve food, and plant and harvest crops. Older children had to care for younger children.

2   Even though they worked very hard, Pilgrim children still had time to play. They probably played marbles, ball games, board games, and running games.

3   Both boys and girls wore gowns (dresses) until they were about seven years old.

4   There was no school in the early years of New Plymouth. Parents taught their children to read and write or had their children taught by neighbors.

5   Children often slept on mattresses that were laid on the floor at night. The mattresses were usually stuffed with straw. Some children slept in their parents' beds.

6   Children and adults probably took baths only a few times a year. At that time, people thought bathing was unhealthy.

1 Paragraph 1 —

    A   describes how Pilgrim children lived
    B   lists ways Pilgrim children helped their parents
    C   explains why neighbors taught Pilgrim children
    D   compares how different Pilgrim families raised their children

2 Pilgrim girls and boys —

    A   rarely bathed
    B   had no time for play
    C   did not learn to read and write
    D   dressed the same until they were adults

15

3   In the early years of the Pilgrim colony, why didn't children go to school?

    A   They thought playing was more fun.
    B   They had too much work to do.
    C   There were no teachers.
    D   There were no schools.

CHOPPING WOOD

1   Two men chopped logs all day. One worked without stopping. The other sat down often. He did not work nearly as hard as his friend did.

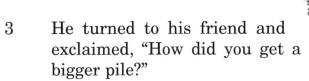

2   At the end of the day, the hard worker had a much smaller pile of wood than did his friend. He was amazed.

3   He turned to his friend and exclaimed, "How did you get a bigger pile?"

4   "Simple," the other replied. "While I was resting, I sharpened my ax."

1   What puzzled the hard worker?

   A   He worked harder but chopped less wood.
   B   He worked all day, but didn't chop any wood.
   C   His friend did no work, but still chopped wood.
   D   His friend was able to chop a lot of wood while sitting down.

2   Why did the hard worker's friend cut more wood?

   A   He worked harder.
   B   He spent more hours chopping wood.
   C   He sharpened his axe while he was resting.
   D   He took wood from the hard worker's pile.

    17

3   The next time he chops wood, the hard worker will probably —

   A   work even harder
   B   work even longer
   C   take another friend with him
   D   make sure his axe stays sharp

4   What lesson does this story teach?

   A   Hard work builds character.
   B   All work and no play make Jack a dull boy.
   C   The harder you work, the more you accomplish.
   D   To do a good job, using your brain is as important as using your muscles.

18

MOUNT ST. HELENS ERUPTS

1   In 1980, Mount St. Helens, in the state of Washington, erupted. Tons of ash and dust flew high into the sky. Thousands and thousands of trees were destroyed. Many animals, birds, and fish were killed.

2   Mount St. Helens is a volcano. A volcano is an opening or vent in the earth. Hot rock from deep inside the earth comes out of the opening. Sometimes ashes explode out of the opening. More often, the melted rock comes up as a red-hot liquid called "lava."

3   A volcano is called an "<u>active</u>" volcano when it is erupting. When the eruptions stop, the volcano is "dormant" or sleeping. A volcano that has not erupted for thousands of years is called "extinct" or finished.

4   Volcanoes are also named for their shapes. The top of a shield volcano looks like a flat shield. It takes many layers of lava to make shield volcanoes. A cinder-cone volcano is shaped like a cone: sharp and narrow on the top, round on the bottom. It is made up of cinders and ash. Cinder-cone volcanoes are usually small.

1 What is Mount St. Helens?

    A A church
    B A mountain
    C A person
    D A volcano

2 What is a volcano?

    A A type of mountain
    B A hole in Earth's surface
    C A type of shield
    D A cone

19

3 Look at the word *active* in paragraph 3. What other word in the paragraph means the same thing?

    A dormant
    B erupting
    C extinct
    D sleeping

4 A cinder cone volcano —

    A is usually very large
    B looks like a flat shield
    C is narrow at the top and made of ash
    D is shaped like a cone and made of lava

5 What usually happens when a volcano erupts?

    A Melted rock comes out of it.
    B There is an earthquake.
    C Cinders shoot out of it.
    D Trees are destroyed.

6 What is this reading about?

    A what happened when Mount St. Helens erupted
    B why volcanoes are called "active" or "dormant"
    C what is in Earth's core
    D volcanos

    20

ANDROCLES AND THE LION

1   In the days of ancient Rome, a slave named Androcles escaped from his master. He ran deep into a forest. There he met a huge lion. Androcles turned to run. Then he noticed that the lion was in great pain. A thorn was wedged into one paw. The paw was swollen and bloody.

2   Androcles came close to the lion. The great beast lay still. The slave then examined the foot. He pulled out the thorn. Androcles wrapped the swollen paw. Soon the lion was better. The grateful beast took Androcles to its lair. The lion brought the man food every day.

3   Early one morning, while the friends were asleep, the lion heard a noise outside his den. He wanted to run away, but waited to wake up Androcles. By the time Androcles awoke, it was too late. They were trapped. Soldiers were outside the cave with nets. The soldiers captured both the slave and his friend, the lion.

4   Androcles was <u>sentenced</u> to die for having run away from his master. In Rome, slaves were killed by being fed to hungry lions in the Coliseum. All of Rome came to the arena where Androcles was to be thrown to the lions.

5   Androcles was very afraid. As he stood in the center of the field, a huge lion came running at him. It was Androcles' old friend!

6   The emperor was amazed when the lion licked Androcles' hand. When he learned the story of the two friends, he pardoned them both saying, "Gratitude is the sign of noble souls."

1   Who was Androcles?

   A   An emperor
   B   A master
   C   A soldier
   D   A slave

21

2   In paragraph 1, why didn't Androcles run away from the lion?

    A   He liked lions.
    B   He didn't see the lion.
    C   He was hungry and wanted to eat the lion.
    D   He saw that the lion was hurt and needed help.

3   Look at these definitions of the word *sentence*.

    1. Jail
    2. Punish
    3. Statement
    4. Stretch

    Which one best explains the meaning of *sentenced* in paragraph 4?

    A   Definition 1
    B   Definition 2
    C   Definition 3
    D   Definition 4

4   In paragraph 6, why didn't the lion eat Androcles?

    A   The lion wasn't hungry.
    B   Androcles killed the lion.
    C   Androcles and the lion were old friends.
    D   The lion didn't like how Androcles tasted.

5   Why did the emperor pardon Androcles and the lion?

    A   How they treated each other proved their goodness.
    B   He was disappointed that the lion didn't eat the man.
    C   Every day, he pardoned one slave who survived.
    D   He was surprised that the lion was friendly.

THE BLIND MEN AND THE ELEPHANT

by John G. Saxe

1 It was six men of Indostan,
  To learning much inclined,
Who went to see the elephant
  (Though all of them were blind)
That each by observation
  Might satisfy his mind.

2 The first approached the elephant
  And, happening to fall
Against his broad and sturdy side,
  At once began to bawl,
"God bless me! But the elephant
  Is very like a wall!"

3 The second, feeling of the tusk,
  Cried, "Ho! What have we here?
So very round and smooth and sharp!
  To me 'tis very clear
This wonder of an elephant
  Is very like a spear!"

4 The third approached the animal
  And, happening to take
The squirming trunk within his hands,
  Thus boldly up he spake:
"I see," <u>quoth</u> he, "the elephant
  Is very like a snake!"

5 The fourth reached out his eager hand,
  And felt about the knee.
"What most this wondrous beast is like
  Is very plain," <u>quoth</u> he;
"'Tis clear enough the elephant
  Is very like a tree!"

6 The fifth, who chanced to touch the ear,
  Said, "E'en the blindest man
Can tell what this resembles most.
  Deny the fact who can:
This marvel of an elephant
  Is very like a fan!"

7   The sixth no sooner had begun
        About the beast to grope
Than, seizing on the swinging tail
        That fell within his scope,
"I see," <u>quoth</u> he, "the elephant
        Is very like a rope!"

8   And so these men of Indostan
        Disputed loud and long,
Each in his own opinion
        Exceeding stiff and strong,
Though each was partly in the right
        And all were in the wrong!

1   The first man describes —

    A   what an elephant looks like
    B   the elephant's side
    C   what he sees
    D   a wall

2   The second man says an elephant is like a —

    A   snake
    B   spear
    C   trunk
    D   tusk

3   Look at the word *quoth* in stanzas 4, 5, and 7. Which of these words means the same thing as *quoth*?

    A   asked
    B   cried
    C   repeated
    D   said

24

4   The six men in the poem —

   A   touch different parts of the elephant
   B   agree on what elephants look like
   C   describe elephants incorrectly
   D   have seen elephants before

5   What is a good example of rhyme?

   A   In stanza 1, "Who <u>went</u> to <u>see</u> the <u>elephant</u>/ (Though <u>all</u> of <u>them</u> were
        <u>blind</u>)"
   B   In stanza 4, "squirming trunk"
   C   In stanza 6, "E'en the blindest man"
   D   In stanza 7, "grope," "scope," and "rope"

6   What lesson does the poem teach?

   A   Elephants are very unusual animals.
   B   Believe only what you see with your own eyes.
   C   You may know a part of the truth without knowing the whole truth.
   D   Never believe what others say because they cannot see the whole truth.

NOTHING BUT A HOUND DOG

1   Ms. Sophie T. Wagglebottom lives in a small house with a large backyard. Whenever she goes into her backyard, she stops right outside the door to sniff the air. Sometimes she will stand for a minute or two with her nose raised high and nostrils spread. Where she goes next often depends on what she smells—and she smells a lot. Sophie, you see, is a basset hound.

2   Basset hounds are scenthounds. They are called *scenthounds* because their noses are very sensitive—much more sensitive than human noses. Over the centuries, scenthounds have worked as hunting and tracking dogs. Some examples are the English foxhound, the American coonhound, and the dachshund. You may have seen movies showing packs of foxhounds chasing foxes and followed by hunters on horseback. Coonhounds were bred in the United States to hunt raccoons. Dachshunds originally came from Germany, where they were used to sniff out badgers.

3   Only one other scenthound has a more sensitive nose than the basset, and that is the bloodhound. Like foxhounds, coonhounds, and dachshunds, early bloodhounds were hunters. They worked alongside their human masters to hunt deer and other animals. Since their noses are so sensitive, today they seldom work as hunting dogs. Instead, they often help police track escaped prisoners, missing people, lost children, and even lost pets. The bloodhound sniffs something that belongs to the person or pet it is looking for and then follows that scent until it finds its target. Bloodhounds are very <u>tenacious</u>, so it is hard to put them off the trail.

4   When Sophie Wagglebottom goes outside, raises her head, and sniffs the morning air, she learns a lot about what is going on around her. She knows what the neighbors are cooking, what fruit fell during the night, and what animals visited her garden while she was asleep. Depending on what she scents, she may head to the neighbors' fence to beg for a bite of sausage or run to the base of the mulberry tree to make sure the raccoon has left the yard. Whatever Sophie does, though, it is her nose that leads the way.

1 What is this reading about?

   A Sophie Wagglebottom
   B Basset hounds
   C Scenthounds
   D Hound dogs

2 Why does Sophie stop outside the door before going into the backyard?

   A She wants to find out what has happened in the yard since she was last there.
   B Since she just got up, she is too tired to run into the yard.
   C She is waiting for her master to catch up to her.
   D She is waiting to be let back into the house.

3 In paragraph 2, why does the author talk about foxhounds, coonhounds, and dachshunds?

   A To show how scenthounds have been used to hunt and track
   B To give examples of the interesting jobs dogs can do
   C To give examples of different types of hounds
   D To explain why hounds make good pets

4 In paragraph 3, what does the word *tenacious* mean?

   A dangerous
   B friendly
   C hungry
   D stubborn

5 Why do the police have bloodhounds working for them?

   A Bloodhounds are stronger than other dogs.
   B Bloodhounds have the best sense of smell.
   C Bloodhounds are very friendly.
   D Bloodhounds are hunting dogs.

27

LOG YOUR SCREEN TIME

1. Did you know that children and teens spend on average 7.5 hours every day using electronic media? Of course, these 7.5 hours include time spent doing homework and watching the family's favorite TV show—but they also include hours of playing games on the computer, surfing the Internet, and just passing time in front of the television.

2. The problem with spending so much time in front of a computer or a TV is that you usually sit down to do it. Sitting still all the time makes people overweight and unhealthy. The human body needs exercise to stay fit. In fact, children need at least one hour of active exercise every day.

3. Are you getting the exercise you need? Or are you one of the "average" children, who spend most of their time sitting still? You can find out by tracking how much "screen time" you have each day on a screen time log like this one.

	TV	Video Games	DVD	Computer/Internet	Total Hours Per Day
MONDAY					
TUESDAY					
WEDNESDAY					
THURSDAY					
FRIDAY					
SATURDAY					
SUNDAY					

TOTAL HOURS PER WEEK ▶

4. Every day, write in how many hours you spend on each of the activities listed on the chart. If your screen time is just one or two hours a day, congratulations! You have a healthy lifestyle. If it is more than that, maybe you should also check your exercise time. If you get less than an hour of exercise a day, start spending more time playing outdoors and doing active chores to help your parents at home.

28

5   You may also want to have other members of your family fill out screen time logs. After all, you want to make sure they stay healthy, too!

1   According to the reading, the average child —

     A   has too much homework to do
     B   spends too much time sitting still
     C   needs more than 7.5 hours of sleep
     D   should get 7.5 hours of exercise every day

2   According to paragraph 2, why should you make sure you exercise every day?

     A   to help your parents with the household chores
     B   to keep yourself busy
     C   to play with friends
     D   to stay healthy

3   What is the purpose of the screen time log?

     A   To show how the average child spends his or her time
     B   To help you calculate how many hours of activity you have each day
     C   To keep a record of the number of hours a week you play video games
     D   To help you find out how much time you spend sitting still every day

4   Based on the information in the text, which of these activities should you do less of?

     A   Homework
     B   Playing soccer
     C   Playing outdoors
     D   Playing video games

5   Based on the information in the text, which of these activities should you do more of?

    A   Homework
    B   Playing soccer
    C   Watching the news
    D   Playing video games

RACCOONS

1   Raccoons are found across most of North America. They have long been common in the eastern United States. In the 1940s, a population explosion occurred. As a result, raccoons expanded their range and their numbers. In the 1980s, there were at least 15 times more raccoons in North America than in the 1930s.

brownish-gray fur

white eyebrows

white, pointed nose

black mask around eyes

fluffy tail with black rings

thin, dextrous front paws

long hind feet

2   Since raccoons are so common, you may have seen one. Their fur is long, dense, and gray-brown in color. They have black face masks and ringed tails. Adult raccoons can be up to three feet long and weigh as much as 30 pounds.

3   Raccoons have long canine teeth, which help them to eat meat. But meat is not the only thing they eat. They also like fruits and vegetables, and they will happily eat pet food left outside. They will even raid people's garbage cans for leftovers.

4   The word *raccoon* comes from an American Indian word, *arakum* or *aracou*, which means, "he scratches with his hands." This is because of raccoons' thin front paws, which are almost like human hands. They use their forepaws to investigate cracks and holes that catch their interest, to catch and hold their food, and to study things they have found. If a raccoon gets curious about a crack in a wall, it will probe it with its forepaws and pull out anything it finds for further inspection. Raccoons hunt for food in or near water or around the edges of crop fields. When they hunt in shallow water, they turn over rocks and tree branches and feel around with their front paws. When a raccoon finds things that look tasty, it examines them by holding them in its front paws and touching them with its nose.

5   With their <u>dexterous</u> forepaws and powerful hind feet, raccoons are excellent climbers. However, like humans and bears, they have flat feet. As a result, they tend to be slow runners.

6   Originally, raccoons tended to live in forested areas, but these intelligent animals have adapted well to <u>urban</u> life. Today, the largest populations are found in cities and towns, where there is plenty of food. They do not build their own dens. Instead, they rely on nature or other animals to do their work for them. In the country, raccoons will often live in hollow trees, old beaver lodges, empty badger dens, or haystacks. In the city, they will happily move into abandoned buildings or old cars. A raccoon will use several dens within its territory. When the weather is cold, raccoons huddle together in group dens for warmth. In hot weather, though, you may find a raccoon relaxing on the ground or sprawled on a large tree limb.

1   Why do raccoons have long canine teeth?

   A   For self-defense
   B   To help them eat meat
   C   To suck juice from fruit
   D   For combing their long fur

2   Between the 1930s and the 1980s, —

   A   The raccoon population boomed.
   B   The number of raccoons dropped.
   C   Raccoons began moving to the cities.
   D   People began feeding raccoons pet food.

3   What color are the markings on a raccoon's tail?

   A   Black
   B   Brown
   C   Gray
   D   White

32

4   Look at the word *dexterous* paragraph 5. It ends in *–ous*. What do you know from that ending?

   A   It is a noun.
   B   It is an adjective.
   C   It expresses ownership.
   D   It compares one thing with another.

5   In paragraph 6, what does the word *urban* mean?

   A   city or town
   B   countryside
   C   forested
   D   rural

6   Which paragraph provides the most evidence that raccoons are highly intelligent?

   A   Paragraph 1
   B   Paragraph 2
   C   Paragraph 4
   D   Paragraph 5

from THE VELVETEEN RABBIT
by Margery Williams

1   Weeks passed, and the little Rabbit grew very old and shabby, but the Boy loved him just as much. He loved him so hard that he loved all his whiskers off, and the pink lining to his ears turned grey, and his brown spots faded. He even began to lose his shape, and he scarcely looked like a rabbit any more, except to the Boy. To the Boy, he was always beautiful, and that was all that the little Rabbit cared about. He didn't mind how he looked to other people, because the nursery magic had made him Real, and when you are Real, shabbiness doesn't matter.

2   And then, one day, the Boy was ill.

3   His face grew very flushed, and he talked in his sleep, and his little body was so hot that it burned the Rabbit when he held him close. Strange people came and went in the nursery, and a light burned all night, and through it all the little Velveteen Rabbit lay there, hidden from sight under the bedclothes, and he never stirred, for he was afraid that if they found him someone might take him away, and he knew that the Boy needed him.

4   It was a long weary time, for the Boy was too ill to play, and the little Rabbit found it rather dull with nothing to do all day long. But he snuggled down patiently, and looked forward to the time when the Boy should be well again, and they would go out in the garden amongst the flowers and the butterflies and play splendid games in the raspberry thicket like they used to. All sorts of delightful things he planned, and while the Boy lay half asleep, he crept up close to the pillow and whispered them in his ear. And presently the fever turned, and the Boy got better. He was able to sit up in bed and look at picture-books, while the little Rabbit cuddled close at his side. And one day, they let the Boy get up and dress.

5   It was a bright, sunny morning, and the windows stood wide open. They had carried the Boy out on to the balcony, wrapped in a shawl, and the little Rabbit lay tangled up among the bedclothes, thinking.

6   The Boy was going to the seaside tomorrow. Everything was arranged, and now it only remained to carry out the doctor's orders. They talked about it all while the little Rabbit lay under the bedclothes, with just his head peeping out, and listened. The room was to be disinfected, and all the books and toys that the Boy had played with in bed must be burnt.

34

7   "Hurrah!" thought the little Rabbit. "Tomorrow we shall go to the seaside!" For the boy had often talked of the seaside, and he wanted very much to see the big waves coming in, and the tiny crabs, and the sand castles.

8   Just then, Nana caught sight of him. "How about his old Bunny?" she asked.

9   "That?" said the doctor. "Why, it's a mass of scarlet fever germs! Burn it at once. Get him a new one. He mustn't have that anymore!"

10   And so the little Rabbit was put into a sack with the old picture-books and a lot of rubbish, and carried out to the end of the garden behind the fowl-house. That was a fine place to make a bonfire, only the gardener was too busy just then to attend to it. He had the potatoes to dig and the green peas to gather, but next morning he promised to come quite early and burn the whole lot.

11   That night the Boy slept in a different bedroom, and he had a new bunny to sleep with him. It was a splendid bunny, all white plush with real glass eyes, but the Boy was too excited to care very much about it. For tomorrow he was going to the seaside, and that in itself was such a wonderful thing that he could think of nothing else.

12   And while the Boy was asleep, dreaming of the seaside, the little Rabbit lay among the old picture-books in the corner behind the fowl-house, and he felt very lonely. The sack had been left untied, and so by wriggling a bit he was able to get his head through the opening and look out. He was shivering a little, for he had always been used to sleeping in a proper bed, and by this time his coat had worn so thin and threadbare from hugging that it was no longer any protection to him. Nearby he could see the thicket of raspberry canes, growing tall and close like a tropical jungle, in whose shadow he had played with the Boy on bygone mornings. He thought of those long sunlit hours in the garden—how happy they were!—and a great sadness came over him. He seemed to see them all pass before him, each more beautiful than the other—the fairy huts in the flower-bed, the quiet evenings in the wood when he lay in the bracken and the little ants ran over his paws, the wonderful day when he first knew that he was Real. He thought of the Skin Horse, so wise and gentle, and all that he had told him. Of what use was it to be loved and lose one's beauty and become Real if it all ended like this? And a tear, a real tear, trickled down his little shabby velvet nose and fell to the ground.

13   And then a strange thing happened. For where the tear had fallen, a flower grew out of the ground—a mysterious flower, not at all like any that grew in the garden. It had slender green leaves the color of emeralds, and in the center of the leaves a blossom like a golden cup. It was so beautiful that the little

     35

Rabbit forgot to cry and just lay there watching it. And presently the blossom opened, and out of it there stepped a fairy.

14   She was quite the loveliest fairy in the whole world. Her dress was of pearl and dew-drops, and there were flowers around her neck and in her hair, and her face was like the most perfect flower of all. And she came close to the little Rabbit and gathered him up in her arms and kissed him on his velveteen nose, which was all damp from crying.

15   "Little Rabbit," she said, "don't you know who I am?" The Rabbit looked up at her, and it seemed to him that he had seen her face before, but he couldn't think where. "I am the nursery magic Fairy," she said. "I take care of all the playthings that the children have loved. When they are old and worn out, and the children don't need them anymore, then I come and take them away with me and turn them into Real."

16   "Wasn't I Real before?" asked the little Rabbit.

17   "You were Real to the Boy," the Fairy said, "because he loved you. Now you shall be Real to everyone."

1   How did the Velveteen Rabbit lose his whiskers and his spots?

   A   He got old.
   B   He became Real.
   C   He was burned in a fire.
   D   The Boy hugged him a lot.

2   In paragraph 3, why is the Boy's body so hot?

   A   He has a fever.
   B   The windows are closed.
   C   He is having a nightmare.
   D   There are too many blankets on the bed.

3   Reread paragraphs 6 and 7. Why do you think the Rabbit expects to go to the seaside and not to be burned?

   A   The Rabbit does not realize he is a toy.
   B   The Boy has promised to take him to the seaside.
   C   He did not hear the adults talking about burning the books and toys.
   D   The doctor has not yet said that he has to be burned with the other toys.

4   Why do the adults take the Rabbit away from the Boy?

   A   The Rabbit is too old.
   B   The Boy won't need the Rabbit at the seaside.
   C   The Rabbit could give the Boy scarlet fever again.
   D   They want to punish the boy for behaving badly.

5   In paragraph 13, the fairy comes from —

   A   the sky
   B   the nursery
   C   a golden cup
   D   a flower that grew from a teardrop

6   In the last paragraph, what does the fairy mean when she says, "You were Real to the Boy"?

   A   The Boy used magic to make the Rabbit Real.
   B   The Boy's feelings made the Rabbit Real to him.
   C   The fairy had made the Rabbit Real, but only to the Boy.
   D   No one but the Boy could see the Rabbit.

7   Do you think that when the Boy comes home from the seaside he will miss the Velveteen Rabbit? Why or why not?

_____

_____

_____

_____

_____

_____

_____

_____

7A Which of the following passages supports the answer you provided to the question above?

A   Weeks passed, and the little Rabbit grew very old and shabby, but the Boy loved him just as much. He loved him so hard that he loved all his whiskers off, and the pink lining to his ears turned grey, and his brown spots faded. He even began to lose his shape, and he scarcely looked like a rabbit any more, except to the Boy. To the Boy, he was always beautiful.

B   The Boy was going to the seaside tomorrow. Everything was arranged, and now it only remained to carry out the doctor's orders. They talked about it all while the little Rabbit lay under the bedclothes, with just his head peeping out, and listened. The room was to be disinfected, and all the books and toys that the Boy had played with in bed must be burnt.

C   "Hurrah!" thought the little Rabbit. "Tomorrow we shall go to the seaside!" For the boy had often talked of the seaside, and he wanted very much to see the big waves coming in, and the tiny crabs, and the sand castles.

D. "That?" said the doctor. "Why, it's a mass of scarlet fever germs! Burn it at once. Get him a new one. He mustn't have that anymore!"

38

ORANGES

1   Oranges are good to eat. They taste tangy and refreshing. They are also good for you. Like all citrus fruits, they have lots of vitamin C, which helps fight disease.

2   Since oranges are so delicious and healthful, you may want to grow an orange tree of your own. If you do, the first thing to do is decide what type of orange tree you want. Do you want a sweet orange or a sour orange? Both are good for making juice. If you don't like seeds, perhaps you would prefer a navel orange. There are also mandarin oranges, like tangerines, and blood oranges, which have red pulp.

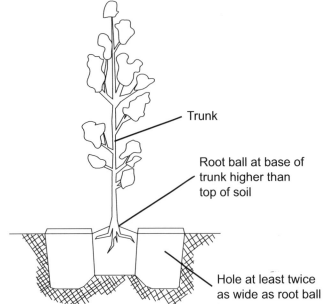

Trunk

Root ball at base of trunk higher than top of soil

Hole at least twice as wide as root ball

3   Once you choose your orange tree and bring it home, you are ready to plant it. You can plant a citrus tree at any time of year. Here's what to do:

    1 Dig a hole that is at least twice as wide as the tree's root ball. Make sure that it is not deeper than the root ball.

    2 Clean the old dirt off the roots of the tree. Make sure that the roots are spread out and not wrapped around each other.

    3 Place the tree in the ground. Then, begin filling in the hole. When you have filled in about half of the hole, water the soil. It will sink a little. This fills in any air pockets that have formed among the roots. When the hole is full, check to make sure the soil does not reach too far up the trunk. At the bottom of the trunk, the very top of the roots should show above the ground.

    4 Water the soil well. The soil may sink a little more. If it does, add some more soil. Except for at the base of the trunk, the roots should be covered completely.

    5 Outside the edges of the hole containing the tree, dig a circle around the tree. This will help keep the water you put on the tree from rolling away from it. Water the tree well.

39

4   For the next few weeks, water twice a week. After that, you do not need to water more than once a week. Watering too often can damage the roots of citrus trees. Fertilize your tree with citrus food according to the instructions on the package.

5   Your new orange tree will flower in spring, and small green fruit will appear a short time later. However, the oranges will not be ripe until the following winter.

1   The title of this reading is too general. What would be a better title?

   A   Fruit
   B   How to Dig a Hole
   C   Planting Fruit Trees
   D   Growing Your Own Oranges

2   Oranges are healthful because they —

   A   taste good
   B   grow on trees
   C   contain vitamin C
   D   are a type of fruit

3   The diagram on page 37 relates to —

   A   paragraph 1
   B   paragraph 2
   C   paragraph 3
   D   paragraph 4

4   After covering the tree's roots with dirt, what should you do next?

    A   Dig a hole.
    B   Water the tree.
    C   Clean the root ball.
    D   Decide what type of oranges you like.

5   Watering a citrus tree every day —

    A   is a good idea
    B   can hurt its roots
    C   will make it grow faster
    D   will make its fruit sweeter

THE ARROW AND THE SONG

by Henry Wadsworth Longfellow

1   I shot an arrow into the air,
      It fell to earth, I knew not where;
      For, so swiftly it flew, the sight
      Could not follow it in its flight.

2   I breathed a song into the air,
      It fell to earth, I knew not where;
      For who has sight so keen and strong,
      That it can follow the flight of song?

3   Long, long afterward, in an oak
      I found the arrow, still unbroke;
      And the song, from beginning to end,
      I found again in the heart of a friend.

1   In verse 1, why couldn't the speaker see where the arrow landed?

A   He didn't look.
B   There were trees in the way.
C   The arrow was flying too fast.
D   He had his eyes closed.

2   In verse 2, why couldn't the speaker see where the song landed?

A   He didn't look.
B   You can't see songs.
C   The song was moving too fast.
D   He didn't have his glasses on.

3   How is the song like the arrow?

   A   The speaker shot both of them into the air with a bow.
   B   Both landed in a tree.
   C   Later, the speaker found both of them undamaged.
   D   Both are invisible.

4   What other two things in the poem are alike?

   A   Earth and air
   B   Sight and flight
   C   Shooting and finding
   D   An oak and a friend's heart

43

CONSTELLATIONS

1   When you look into the night sky, you see hundreds of stars. There are so many stars that nobody can count them all. Sometimes groups of stars seem to make pictures in the sky. These sky pictures are called constellations. If you look carefully, you may be able to see some constellations. You will have to use more than just your eyes, though. You will also have to use your imagination.

2   One of the easiest constellations to find is the Big Dipper. It has the shape of a small pan with a long handle. Look for it on starry nights. Two of the stars in the Big Dipper point to the North Star. The North Star is almost directly above the North Pole. Travelers use the North Star to find out which way is north.

Orion, the Hunter, and Canis Major

3   Another constellation is Orion. Orion looks like a hunter. He holds a club in one hand and a lion skin in the other. His belt is easy to find in the sky. It is made of three stars in a row. The three stars in Orion's belt point to a star called Sirius. Sirius, sometimes called the Dog Star, is the brightest star in the sky.

4   Sirius gets its name because it is in another constellation, Canis Major. Canis Major means "Big Dog" in Latin. This constellation is one of Orion's two hunting dogs.

5   Many constellations are names for animals. Some examples are Pegasus, the winged horse; Lepus, the hare; Lupus, the wolf; Monoceros, the unicorn; and Scorpius, the scorpion. In fact, the Big Dipper has an animal name, too—Ursa Major, or the "Great Bear."

44

1 Constellations are made of —

   A animals
   B images
   C imagination
   D stars

2 People use the North Star to —

   A find the Big Dipper
   B locate Orion's belt
   C see which way is north
   D find the brightest star in the sky

3 The picture does not relate to —

   A Paragraph 1
   B Paragraph 2
   C Paragraph 3
   D Paragraph 4

4 Which constellation mentioned in the text does not have an animal name?

   A Big Dipper
   B Canis Major
   C Orion
   D Ursa Major

5   You need to use your imagination to see —

    A   the shapes the constellations are named for
    B   why Sirius is called the Dog Star
    C   the stars in the night sky
    D   the North Star

KILLER WHALE

1   Did you know that killer whales are not whales at all? They are dolphins. Originally, Spanish whalers called them "whale killers." The killer whale's scientific name is Orcinus orca. Like all dolphins, the killer whale is a mammal.

2   The killer whale is found in all of the world's oceans. Usually they live in cooler, deeper waters. Males can grow to about 32 feet in length. They can weigh up to 10 tons. Females can grow to 27 feet in length. They can weigh up to seven tons. Newborn calves are about seven feet in length. At birth they weigh almost 400 pounds.

3   Killer whales can travel from 60 to 100 miles of ocean a day. They use echoes for navigation and for finding food. This is called "echolocation." They often hunt in packs. Food items for the killer whale include squid, fish, skates, rays, sharks, sea turtles, sea birds, seals, sea lions, and walrus, as well as large whales, e.g., fin whales, humpback whales, right whales, and gray whales. They have also been known to attack the sperm whale and the blue whale.

4   Orcas live in pods of up to 50 members. Within these pods are smaller units called subpods. Orcas stay with their subpods all their lives.

5   Common killer whale behavior includes:

- Spyhopping: The orca stands on its tail and brings its head out of the water.
- Breaching: The killer whale completely leaps out of the water and, as it hits the surface of the water, it lands with an immense explosion.
- Lobtailing: The orca slaps its tail in the water in an interesting display, showing that it interprets something nearby as a possible threat.
- Slapping: The orca slaps its flippers against the surface of the water, possibly to attract fish.

6   Researchers have currently identified up to 62 separate sounds produced by orcas underwater; these include squeaks, chirps, and whistles.

47

1 Killer whales are

    A dolphins
    B right whales
    C fin whales
    D humpback whales

2 Spanish whalers probably called these animals "whale killers" because they —

    A look like whales
    B are whales that kill
    C sometimes kill and eat whales
    D behave like other types of whales

3 Which of these statements about killer whales is not true?

    A They spend their lives alone.
    B They squeak, chirp, and whistle.
    C They eat many other types of animals.
    D They use echolocation to find their way around the oceans.

4 What do we call a group of killer whales who live together?

    A Clan
    B Family
    C Genus
    D Pod

5   The abbreviation "*e.g.*" in paragraph 3 means —

A   every good thing
B   for example
C   and so on
D   except

6   Why might a killer whale slap its tail on the water?

A   To attract fish
B   In response to danger
C   To play with its pod members
D   As part of an attack on other whales

OUR OLDEST PUBLIC SCHOOL

1   The oldest public school in the United States is the Boston Latin School. Puritans founded it in 1635. That was just five years after they founded the city of Boston. At first, students had classes in the schoolmaster's home. Ten years later, a schoolhouse was built in School Street.

2   Students went to the school for seven years. It prepared them to study at a university. From the beginning, the Boston Latin School was open to all boys, whether rich or poor. At that time, it was normal for people to pay for their children's education. This school was different. The colony used tax money to run it.

3   Many famous Americans were pupils at the Boston Latin School. One of these was John Hancock, the first person to sign the Declaration of Independence. Another was Benjamin Franklin, who had to drop out after just one year, when he was 10. More recently, Joseph Kennedy—the father of President John Kennedy—went to school there. So did the famous U.S. composer Leonard Bernstein.

4   It took a long time for the Boston Latin School to become coeducational. It did not accept girl students until 1972.

1   The Puritans probably —

    A   wanted to declare independence from England
    B   did not have time to educate their children
    C   believed that education is important
    D   did not believe in paying taxes

2   Poor boys could go to the Boston Latin School because —

    A   taxes paid fo   r it
    B   their parents paid for it
    C   the schoolmaster paid for it
    D   Puritans lent their parents money

50

3   Which paragraph explains what a public school is?

    A   Paragraph 1
    B   Paragraph 2
    C   Paragraph 3
    D   Paragraph 4

4   Paragraph 3 —

    A   gives examples of famous Boston Latin School students
    B   explains why the Boston Latin School is famous
    C   tells why Benjamin Franklin dropped out
    D   describes what students studied

5   Reread paragraph 4. The word *coeducational* means —

    A   having both male and female students
    B   having two different schools
    C   having only female pupils
    D   the same as educational

A BOOK

by Emily Dickinson

1	He ate and drank the precious words,
2	His spirit grew robust;
3	He knew no more that he was poor,
4	Nor that his frame was dust.
5	He danced along the dingy days,
6	And this bequest of wings
7	Was but a book. What liberty
8	A loosened spirit brings!

1   In lines 1 and 2, the speaker says that —

   A   words cost a lot of money
   B   books are important and valuable
   C   "he" is so hungry that he eats a book
   D   words feed the spirit like food feeds the body

2   In the poem, which words are a good example of alliteration?

   A   "He ate and drank the precious words"
   B   "robust" – "dust"
   C   "more" – "poor"
   D   "danced along the dingy days"

3   The person the poem describes is probably —

   A   a child
   B   a minister
   C   old and poor
   D   an energetic dancer

52

4   According to the poem, —

    A   books strengthen and free the mind
    B   people need to escape their daily lives
    C   if you are hungry, you will find food somewhere
    D   sticks and stones may break your bones, but words will never hurt you

WHAT ARE SPRAINS AND STRAINS?

What Is a Sprain?

1 A sprain is an injury to a ligament (tissue that connects two or more bones at a joint). In a sprain, one or more ligaments is stretched or torn.

What Causes a Sprain?

2 Many things can cause a sprain. Falling, twisting, or getting hit can force a joint out of its normal position. This can cause ligaments around the joint to stretch or tear. Sprains can occur if a person:

- falls and lands on an arm;
- falls on the side of his or her foot; or
- twists a knee.

Where Do Sprains Usually Occur?

3 Sprains happen most often in the ankle. Sometimes when people fall and land on their hands, they sprain their wrists. A sprain to the thumb is common in skiing and other sports.

What Are the Signs and Symptoms of Sprains?

4 The usual signs and symptoms of a sprain are:

- pain;
- swelling;
- bruising; and
- not being able to move or use the joint.

Sometimes people feel a pop or tear when the injury happens. A sprain can be mild, moderate, or severe.

What Is a Strain?

5 A strain is an injury to a muscle or a tendon (tissue that connects muscle to bone). In a strain, a muscle or tendon is stretched or torn.

What Causes Strains?

6 A strain is caused by twisting or pulling a muscle or tendon. Strains can happen suddenly or develop over days or weeks.

54

A sudden (acute) strain is caused by:

- a recent injury;
- lifting heavy objects the wrong way; or
- overstressing the muscles.

7   Chronic strains are usually caused by moving the muscles and tendons the same way over and over.

Where Do Strains Usually Occur?

8   Two common sites for a strain are the back and the hamstring muscle in the back of the thigh. Sports such as soccer, football, hockey, boxing, and wrestling put people at risk for strains in the back or legs. Sports that require people to use their hands or arms a lot can cause strains to hands, arms or elbows. These sports include gymnastics, tennis, rowing and golf.

What Are the Signs and Symptoms of Strains?

9   A strain can cause:

- pain;
- muscle spasms;
- muscle weakness;
- swelling;
- cramping; or
- trouble moving the muscle.

If a muscle or tendon is torn completely, it is often very painful and hard to move.

How Are Sprains and Strains Treated?

10   Treatments for sprains and strains are the same. To reduce swelling and pain in the first day or two, doctors usually say to:

- Rest the injured area. If the ankle or knee is hurt, the doctor might tell you to use crutches or a cane.
- Put ice on the injury for 20 minutes at a time.
- Compress (squeeze) the injury using special bandages, casts, boots, or splints. Your doctor will tell you which one is best for you.
- Put the injured ankle, knee, elbow, or wrist up on a pillow.
- Take medicines, such as aspirin or ibuprofen.

11   After treating pain and swelling, doctors usually say to exercise the injured area. This helps to prevent stiffness and increase strength. Some people need physical therapy. You may need to exercise the injured area or go to physical therapy for several weeks. Your doctor or physical therapist will tell you when you can start to do normal activities, including sports. If you begin too soon, you can injure the area again. It is important to see a doctor if you have a painful sprain or strain. This helps you get the right treatment.

Can Sprains and Strains Be Prevented?

12   To help prevent sprains and strains, you can:

- Avoid exercising or playing sports when tired or in pain.
- Eat a well-balanced diet to keep muscles strong.
- Maintain a healthy weight.
- Try to avoid falling. (For example, put sand or salt on icy spots on your front steps or sidewalks.)
- Wear shoes that fit well.
- Get new shoes if the heel wears down on one side.
- Exercise every day.
- Be in proper physical condition to play a sport.
- Warm up and stretch before playing a sport.
- Wear protective equipment when playing.
- Run on flat surfaces.

1   Paragraph 2 —

    A lists examples of types of sprains
    B explains how sprains and strains differ
    C lists and explains different causes of sprains
    D lists activities to avoid so you won't get a sprain

2   How do sprains differ from strains?

    A Sprains cause swelling; strains do not.
    B In sprains, the ligament is stretched; in strains, it is torn.
    C Sprains usually affect your ankle, but strains affect your arms.
    D Sprains affect ligaments, while strains affect tendons or muscles.

3 You may have a sprain if —

A your arm is bruised
B your ankle is swollen
C you have a terrible headache
D you keep getting cramps in your hand

4 In paragraph 8, what does the word *sites* mean?

A medicines
B pains
C places
D visions

5 If you strain your back —

A don't move it until the strain has healed
B lie in bed with your back on a pillow
C take aspirin or other medicine
D walk with a cane

57

THE LITTLE SHEPHERD BOY

1　Once upon a time, there was a little shepherd boy who was famed far and wide for the wise answers he gave to all questions. When the King of the country heard of the boy, he did not believe what was said about him, so he ordered the boy to come to court. When the boy arrived, the King said to him, "If you can answer three questions, I will bring you up as my own child, and you will live here with me in my palace."

2　"What are these three questions?" asked the boy.

3　"The first is this: How many drops of water are there in the sea?"

4　"My lord King," replied the shepherd boy, "let all the waters be brought up on the earth so that not one drop runs into the sea before I can count it. Then I will tell you how many drops there are in the sea."

5　"The second question," said the King, "is this: How many stars are there in the sky?"

6　"Give me a large sheet of paper," said the boy. Then he took a pin and made so many tiny holes in the paper that they dazzled the eyes of anyone who looked at them. The holes were far too <u>numerous</u> to see or to count. This done, the boy said, "There are as many stars in the sky as there are holes in this paper. Now count them." But nobody could.

7　Then, the King said: "The third question is this: How many seconds are there in eternity?"

8　"In Lower Pomerania there is a mountain. It is one mile in height, one mile in width, and one mile deep. Once in every thousand years, a bird comes to the mountain and rubs its beak against it. When the bird has rubbed the whole mountain away, the first second of eternity will have passed."

9　"You have answered the three questions wisely," said the King. "From now on, you will live with me in my palace, and I will treat you as my own child."

58

1   The King wants to meet the shepherd boy in order to —

A   adopt him
B   test his wisdom
C   buy some sheep's cheese
D   ask his advice on running the kingdom

2   Why doesn't the boy give the King exact answers?

A   The three questions are impossible to answer.
B   The King doesn't give the boy enough time.
C   The boy doesn't want to live with the King.
D   The boy isn't good at math.

3   Which of these statements about the boy's answers is true?

A   They are wrong.
B   They show he is not really wise.
C   They help the King calculate the answers himself.
D   They show why it is impossible to give exact answers to the questions.

4   The word *numerous* in paragraph 6 is probably related to the word —

A   joyous
B   new
C   number
D   star

THE BEST REPORTER IN THE WORLD

1   Nellie Bly was one of the first female news reporters. Nellie began her career in 1882, when she was only 18. Before she got her start in journalism, she was simply an opinionated citizen. Upset by a letter to the editor published in a newspaper, Nellie wrote a letter of her own in reply. Nellie's letter angrily stated that she thought the first letter was unfair to women. She did not sign the letter using her own name, so the editor of the newspaper did not know who wrote it. However, he was so impressed with the writing in the letter, that he placed an ad in the newspaper asking the author of the letter to come into the newsroom.

2   The next day, Nellie climbed four flights of stairs to the newsroom of the *Pittsburgh Dispatch* to meet the editor. She was asked to write an article and then was hired as a reporter.

3   Nellie tried to help people through her writing. She specialized in going undercover. This meant that she pretended to be someone else to find out what was really going on. Nellie put her undercover skills to work to <u>reveal</u> poor working conditions throughout the city. She once pretended to be sick so she could stay in a hospital. She had heard that patients were mistreated there—and she was right. By writing about her experiences for the newspaper, Nellie exposed abuse the patients suffered. When people read about the patient abuse, they became angry and the hospital was forced to change its ways. Another time, Nellie got herself arrested. She wanted to be thrown into jail so she could see how women prisoners were treated and write about it.

4   In time, Nellie was sent to Mexico where she wrote a series of articles about the way people there were forced to live in poverty. Her articles got so much attention that Mexican officials asked her to leave the country! Nellie returned to the United States, this time to New York City, where she landed a job as a reporter for the *New York World*. Her excellent writing made her a celebrity. She became known as "the best reporter in the world."

5   Nellie was also famous for her adventurous spirit. Later in her life, she read a popular book, *Around the World in 80 Days*, in which a make-believe character travels the world, setting a record for doing so in only 80 days. Nellie decided to break this record. She traveled, mainly by steamboat, at a furious pace. Up until this time, no man or woman had ever made this trip so quickly. Nellie broke the character's record: she traveled the world in only 72 days. When she returned to the United States, she was honored with a parade and fireworks.

60

1 According to paragraph 1, why did the newspaper editor want to hire Nellie Bly?

   A She had more experience than the others who applied for the job.
   B Her reply to a letter published in the newspaper was very well written.
   C She had traveled around the world, so she knew about a lot of different countries.
   D Because she was young, he knew he would not have to pay her very much.

2 This text —

   A explains what newspaper reporters do
   B describes Nellie Bly's trip around the world
   C explains why people were angry with Nellie Bly
   D describes Nellie Bly's career as a news reporter

3 Look at the word *reveal* in paragraph 3. What other word in the paragraph means the same thing?

   A expose
   B help
   C pretend
   D suffer

4 What best explains the purpose of paragraph 3?

   A To give reasons why working conditions were poor
   B To list Nellie Bly's solutions to problems in the city
   C To describe examples of Nellie Bly's undercover activities
   D To explain why people became angry at the hospital's treatment of patients

61

5   Which of the following best describes Nellie Bly?

    A brave and caring
    B careful and frightened
    C angry and adventurous
    D young and inexperienced

6   According to the text, why did Nellie Bly decide to travel around the world?

    A She wanted to report on poverty in another country.
    B No woman had ever traveled around the world before.
    C She wanted to break the record set in a popular novel.
    D She hoped that it would make her famous.

WEBPAGE: BRANCHES OF GOVERNMENT

Branches of Government

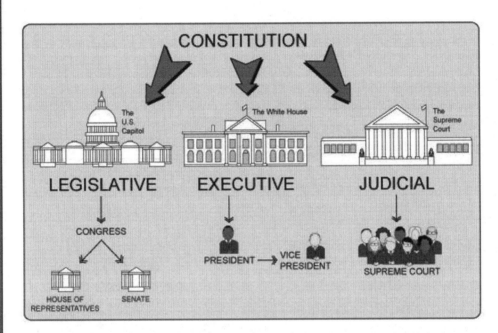

The <u>Founding Fathers</u>, the framers of the <u>Constitution</u>, wanted to form a government that did not allow one person to have too much authority or control. While under the rule of the British king they learned that this could be a bad system. Yet government under the <u>Articles of Confederation</u> taught them that there was a need for a strong centralized government.

With this in mind the framers wrote the Constitution to provide for a <u>separation of powers</u>, or three separate branches of government. Each has its own responsibilities and at the same time they work together to make the country run smoothly and to assure that the rights of citizens are not ignored or disallowed. This is done through <u>checks and balances</u>. A branch may use its powers to check the powers of the other two in order to maintain a balance of power among the three branches of government.

The three branches of the U.S. Government are the legislative, executive, and judicial. A complete diagram of the branches of the U.S. Government may be found in the <u>U.S. Government Manual</u> (PDF).

To learn more, choose from the following:

- *Branches of Government*
- <u>Legislative Branch</u>
- <u>Executive Branch</u>
- <u>Judicial Branch</u>

A service of the Superintendent of Documents, <u>U.S. Government Printing Office</u>.

Source: Ben's Guide to U.S. Government for Kids, U.S. Government Printing Office (bensguide.gpo.gov).

1   The legislative, executive, and judicial are —

    A   the three branches of the U.S. Government
    B   the Articles of Confederation
    C   checks and balances
    D   Congress

2   According to the chart, the Senate is in the —

    A   House of Representatives
    B   legislative branch
    C   executive branch
    D   judicial branch

3   How can you see a more complete version of the chart?

    A   By clicking on the chart
    B   By visiting another Web page
    C   By downloading the U.S. Government Manual
    D   By clicking the link to the U.S. Government Printing Office

4   In the first line of the text, the word "Constitution" is underlined. What would
    probably happen if you clicked on that word?

    A   The picture on the page would change.
    B   A drop-down list of options would appear.
    C   A definition of the word Constitution would appear in a box.
    D   Another page would open showing the U.S. Constitution.

THE PIED PIPER – PART I

by Florence Holbrook

Characters: *Mayor, First Councilman, Second Councilman, Third Councilman, Ten Citizens, Piper*

Scene I: The Mayor's Office

(Mayor and Councilmen, sitting around a table. Citizens come in.)

First Citizen: Our Mayor is useless!

Second Citizen: Look at our town council sitting in the fine clothes we pay for and doing nothing!

Third Citizen: See here! The rats made a nest in my Sunday hat!

Fourth Citizen: When I was cooking dinner, the bold rats licked the soup from my ladle!

Fifth Citizen: They are so bold that they are always fighting with the dogs and cats!

Sixth Citizen: Yes, and they kill them, too!

Seventh Citizen: My baby cried in his sleep, and when I went to him, there was a big rat in his cradle.

Eighth Citizen: What are you going to do about it, Mr. Mayor?

Ninth Citizen: You'd better wake up, sirs! Don't go to sleep over this!

Tenth Citizen: I tell you, you have to do something to save us from this army of rats!

First Councilman: What can we do?

Second Councilman: I'm sure we've tried everything, but every day the rats grow worse and worse.

Third Councilman: It isn't very nice for us to have a town overrun with rats!

Mayor: It is no easy thing to be mayor. I wish I was a plowboy in the country! Try to think of something to do.

First Councilman: It's easy for you to tell us to find a solution!

Second Councilman: I'm sure my head aches trying to think.

Third Councilman: I've thought and thought till I have no thoughts left.

Mayor: If I only had a great big trap! Or, better yet, a thousand big traps! *(Someone knocks on the door.)* What made that noise? Is it a rat?

(Enter Piper.)

First Councilman: Who dares to come into the Mayor's office without an introduction?

Second Councilman: Doesn't he have a funny coat on?

Third Councilman: But what a pleasant face! He smiles all the time.

Mayor: He looks like the picture of my grandfather. What is your name, and what is your business, my man?

Piper: Please, your honors, my name is Piper. My business is to play upon my pipe. With the magic of my notes, I can make all things do my will. But I use my magic on creatures that do people harm—toads, moles, and vipers—and of course, rats.

Mayor: Rats! Well, then, you're the man we want. We'll pay you a thousand guilders if you'll free our town of rats.

Piper: A thousand guilders! Done! It's a deal!

---

1   What problem does the town have?

   A   A bad mayor
   B   High taxes
   C   Pipers
   D   Rats

2　Whom do the citizens blame for their problem?

   A　The town council
   B　Themselves
   C　The Piper
   D　The rats

3　The Mayor's office is —

   A　big
   B　on a river bank
   C　on the fourth floor
   D　the setting for the play

4　In this scene, the Mayor and Councilmen can best be described as —

   A　evil
   B　helpless
   C　intelligent
   D　young

5　If the Piper gets rid of the rats —

   A　the town will pay him a thousand guilders
   B　the Mayor will learn to play a pipe
   C　the children will miss their pets
   D　the citizens will be angry

THE PIED PIPER – PART II
by Florence Holbrook

Scene II—Same as Scene I.

(The Mayor and Councilmen looking out of window)

Mayor: There he goes down the street.

First Councilman: What a strange looking pipe he plays!

Second Councilman: I believe it must be a magic one.

Third Councilman: Do you hear the music? What's that other noise?

Mayor: Look, look at the rats! Did you ever see such a sight!

First Councilman: The streets are crowded with them! Big and little, brown and gray—they're tumbling over each other in their hurry!

Second Councilman: He's going toward the bridge.

Third Councilman: They must think he is playing a tune of apples and cheese!

Mayor: There they are at the river. The rats are plunging in! They'll all be drowned!

First Councilman: Good for the piper!

Mayor: Ring the bells for the people. Tell them to get long poles and poke out the rats' nests! Tell them to block up the rats' holes!

Second Councilman: Here comes the Piper.

Third Councilman: That was well done, Mr. Piper.

Pied Piper: Yes, all the rats are drowned, and now I've come for my pay.

Mayor: Pay! Why? What have you done? Just played a tune on your pipe. You must be joking.

Piper: You promised!

First Councilman: You impudent fellow! You certainly don't think a tune on your pipe is worth one thousand guilders? There is no work in playing a little ditty.

Second Councilman: The rats are dead. I don't think they'll come to life again.

Mayor: My friend, we are much obliged, of course. We are much obliged and will gladly give you fifty guilders. You know your time is not worth more.

Piper: I'll have what you promised, or you may find I'll play a tune you do not like!

Mayor: What? Do you threaten us, fellow? Do what you please. Do you think we care? Play whatever tune you wish on your old pipe.

Piper: Listen, then, and watch from your window when I play again in the street below. *(Goes out.)*

Mayor: What does the lazy fellow mean?

First Councilman: Hear that wonderful music! Listen.

Second Councilman: No! What is he doing? Look at the children!

Third Councilman: They're following him. There's my son. Where are you going, my boy? Come back!

Mayor: Let me see! O woe! there are my own three lovely children. Run, someone, and stop them!

Third Councilman: I'll go, I'll go. (Runs out.)

Mayor: It's useless. Every child in our city is following the magic sound.

Second Councilman: The music seems to be saying, "Come, children, to the wonderful land of play. Flowers and fruits will welcome you. The birds and beasts will play with you, and you will never be sad or sorry in the wonderful land of play." No wonder the children are following the Piper!

Third Councilman (*enters*): The children and the Piper have all disappeared. A mountain opened and let them in.

First Councilman: Our children, our darling children, have gone! What shall we do without the children?

Mayor: Oh, what a wicked man I am! Why did I break my promise? Why did I not give him the thousand guilders?

Second Councilman: Yes, we are all wicked men, and we have been punished.

Mayor: Let us write this sad story where all may read it, and let us paint a picture of the Piper with our little ones following him on a church window, so all men may know how our children were stolen away.

1   Why do the characters describe what is happening in the street?

   A   Each one sees something different.
   B   The audience can't see the street.
   C   They are playing a game.
   D   They don't trust the Piper.

2   Why do the rats go into the river?

   A   They are thirsty.
   B   The citizens are chasing them.
   C   The Piper's magic makes them do it.
   D   They think there are apples and cheese in the river.

3   In this scene, the Mayor is —

   A   clever
   B   dishonest
   C   friendly
   D   polite

4   How does the Piper punish the town for not paying him?

    A   He takes away their children.
    B   He refuses to play his pipe.
    C   He steals all their money.
    D   He drowns their rats.

5   What lesson does the play teach?

    A   Rats are dangerous.
    B   Pipers are dangerous.
    C   Be polite to strangers.
    D   People should keep their word.

71

OUR SOLAR SYSTEM

1   Earth is one of eight planets orbiting the Sun. The Sun and its eight planets, as well as dwarf planets, moons, and various small bodies form our solar system. The moons in the solar system orbit other bodies, like our Moon orbits Earth. As Earth and other bodies move around the sun, their moons travel with them. Small bodies also orbit the sun. The term small bodies refers to asteroids, comets, and meteoroids.

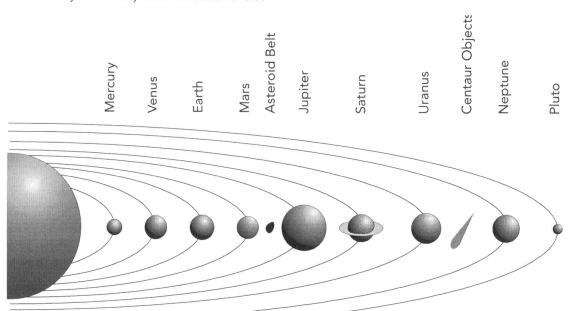

2

The drawing above shows the sun, the planets, an asteroid, a comet, and Pluto. Pluto is one of the dwarf planets in the Kuiper belt. The Kuiper belt also includes other objects, like comets. Kuiper belt objects are made of rock and ice. They orbit the sun in one of two ways—in a circular path or in an <u>elongated</u> path. Sometimes, other forces may act on the objects travelling in an elongated path, making them leave the Kuiper belt. For example, the Sun's gravity might pull them closer to the center of the solar system. This may explain how the Centaur objects came into orbit between Jupiter and Neptune.

3   The solar system contains several hundred thousand asteroids. Most of them orbit the sun in the asteroid belt. Like comets, their orbits are not circular, and they sometimes come close to Earth.

4   Asteroids are made of rock, of metal, or of rock and metal. Most meteoroids are probably pieces of asteroids. They are quite small. When they come near Earth, these small objects can be pulled in by Earth's gravity. When meteoroids enter Earth's atmosphere, they burn up, creating what we call falling stars, or meteors. Some do not burn completely, but reach Earth's surface. These are called meteorites. Most meteorites fall into the ocean, but

72

a few hit solid ground. Scientists learn about other bodies in our solar system by examining these meteorites.

5   The diagram of our solar system is not really complete. Far beyond Pluto is the huge Oort cloud, which contains icy bodies, like comets. All of these bodies are also orbiting our Sun. The Oort cloud surrounds our solar system and reaches far into space.

1   Our solar system contains —

A   the Sun and nine planets
B   the Sun, the Earth, and the Moon
C   the Sun, the planets, and the dwarf planets
D   the Sun, the planets, moons, and many other things

2   Which of the following is true?

A   Moons orbit the Sun.
B   Only Earth has a moon.
C   Moons only orbit planets.
D   Moons travel with the bodies they orbit.

3   Look at the word *elongated* in paragraph 2. What root word in *elongated* helps you to know what it means?

A   E–
B   Long
C   Gate
D   –ed

4   Why can scientists learn about asteroids from studying meteorites?

    A Meteorites come from comets, which are similar to asteroids.
    B Meteors are asteroids that fall through Earth's atmosphere.
    C Meteorites are made of metal and rock, like asteroids.
    D Most meteorites are pieces of asteroids.

5   Where is the asteroid belt?

    A In Earth's atmosphere
    B Between Mars and Jupiter
    C Between Jupiter and Neptune
    D Beyond the Kuiper belt

6   Paragraph 3 —

    A explains what asteroids are
    B gives examples of asteroids
    C compares asteroids and comets
    D explains what causes asteroids to leave orbit

THE BROOK

By Alfred, Lord Tennyson

1   I come from haunts of coot and hern,*
        I make sudden sally
        And sparkle out among the fern,
        To bicker down a valley.

2   By thirty hills I hurry down,
        Or slip between the ridges,
        By twenty thorps, a little town,
        And half a hundred bridges.

3   I chatter over stony ways,
        In little sharps and trebles,
        I bubble into eddying bays,
        I babble on the pebbles.

4   With many a curve my banks I fret
        By many a field and fallow,
        And many a fairy foreland set
        With willow-weed and mallow.

5   And here and there a foamy lake
        Upon me, as I travel
        With many a silvery waterbreak
        Above the golden gravel,

6   And draw them all along, and flow
        To join the brimming river,
        For men may come and men may go,
        But I go on forever.

* **"coot and hern"** These are water birds; the word *hern* is a short form of *heron*.

1   Some words in the poem imitate the sound the brook makes as it flows. What are some examples?

    A Bicker, chatter, babble
    B Eddying, foamy, brimming
    C Haunts, curve, travel
    D Sally, sparkle, slip

2   Reread the first line of the poem. In the poem, who is "I"—that is, who is speaking?

    A A bird
    B A brook
    C The poet
    D Someone watching a brook flowing by

3   From reading the poem, we know that—

    A the brook is quite long
    B the brook has dried up
    C many men fish in the brook
    D the brook flows into the ocean

4   The brook is different from people because —

    A it talks all the time
    B it passes many towns
    C people's lives are short
    D people don't travel as far

DECISIONS, DECISIONS

1   We make decisions every day of our lives. It starts before we get out of bed in the morning. Should I get up now, or should I sleep a little longer? As soon as we get up, there are many more things to decide. What shall I wear? What do I want for breakfast? Where shall I sit on the bus? Should I raise my hand to answer the teacher's question? Who should I sit with at lunch? What book do I want from the library? The list goes on and on.

2   Some decisions are unimportant, so we hardly notice them. Others are very important, and it is these big decisions that are not always easy to make. That's why some people come up with aids to help them make big decisions.

3   One method is to list "pros" and "cons." Pros are advantages, and cons are disadvantages. For example, let's say you have to choose between (1) doing your homework right after school and (2) playing baseball with your friends after school. To help you make a decision between the two options, you can make a list of the pros and cons of each. Your list might look like this:

DO HOMEWORK AFTER SCHOOL		PLAY BASEBALL AFTER SCHOOL	
Pros	Cons	Pros	Cons
1. More time to do homework 2. Will be ready for quiz 3. <u>Time for TV</u>	1. No time to see friends 2. No exercise	1. Time with friends 2. Lots of exercise	1. May not have time to finish homework 2. May not be ready for quiz 3. No time for TV

4   After making your list, look at how many pros and cons you have under each option. Then, underline the most important of the pros. If the longest list of pros also contains the most important pro, then you should probably decide for that option. For instance, here, doing homework after school has more pros than playing baseball. If you also underlined "Time for TV" as the most important pro, you should probably decide to do your homework right after school.

5   Another decision-making strategy is to make a decision tree. A decision tree helps you analyze the possible results of your decision. You have to ask yourself, "If I choose to do X, what will happen?" and then "What will happen after that?" Fill in your predictions on a diagram like this:

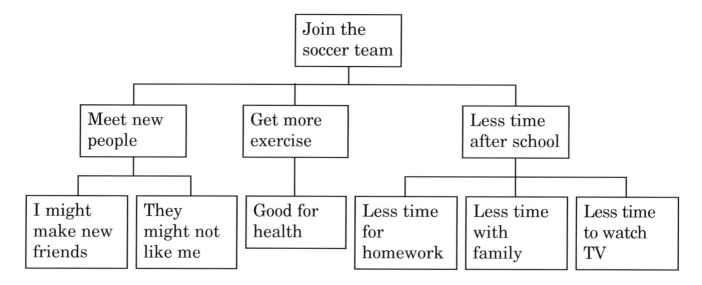

6   As you can see, decision trees are more detailed and require more thought than listing pros and cons.

7   These are just two of the many tools to help people make decisions. Of course, for most of the decisions we make, we don't need tools like this. Still, using such tools can sometimes help prevent us from making the wrong decision.

1   This text —

    A   defines the word decision
    B   explains how to make the right decision
    C   introduces tools to help you make important decisions
    D   examines why people do not like to make big decisions

2   In paragraph 3, what is the meaning of the word *options*?

    A   Advantages
    B   Choices
    C   Methods
    D   Opportunities

3   According to the text —

    A   people do not often have to make decisions
    B   everyone finds it difficult to make decisions
    C   no one makes decisions effectively
    D   people make decisions all day long

4   A decision tree —

    A   lists pros and cons
    B   has a lot of branches
    C   helps you predict the effects of your decisions
    D   helps you recognize the advantages and disadvantages of your decisions

5   Look at the table listing pros and cons about after-school activities. Why is "Time for TV" underlined?

    A   It is the most important advantage to playing baseball after school.
    B   It is the worst disadvantage to playing baseball after school.
    C   It is the most important advantage to doing homework after school.
    D   It is the worst disadvantage to doing homework after school.

6   Underlining "Time for TV" in the table is —

    A   an example of the process described in paragraph 3
    B   an example of the process described in paragraph 4
    C   an example of a disadvantage
    D   an example of a decision tree

79

DR. SMITHERS IN THE BASEMENT

1   Last summer, Dr. Smithers moved into the old house next door. Dr. Smithers had gray hair that stood straight up. He had a lot of wrinkles on his face and he walked with a cane. No one knew what kind of doctor he was. He never had any visitors. No one knew quite what to make of him.

2   At night, we could see his basement light on, but no one knew what he was doing. One night, a big, black car pulled up in front of the house and some people carried a large object inside. It was too dark to see what it was, but I had my suspicions. I had just seen a movie about Frankenstein. I was beginning to develop my own theory about Dr. Smithers.

3   Dr. Smithers had a strange housekeeper named Mildred. Mildred dressed in black and spoke with a foreign accent. One day, I went to Dr. Smithers's house. I was determined to find out what went on in the basement. Mildred would not let me in. She said that damp weather had <u>aggravated</u> Dr. Smithers's arthritis and that he was in bed. However, as I left I saw him watching me through the window. I went around to the other side of the house, examining the basement windows, and I knew what I had to do.

4   I decided that I would sneak into Dr. Smithers's basement to find out what he did there. I waited for a night when Dr. Smithers was not working in the basement. One night, I saw that the basement lights were out. I climbed in through a window. I found a machine and a large assortment of rocks. Some of the rocks were shiny, as if they had been polished. How could I have been so wrong about Dr. Smithers's hobby?

5   I stood in Dr. Smithers's basement, feeling embarrassed that I had suspected him of creating Frankenstein monsters. I heard the sound of a cane at the top of the basement stairs. I knew it was Dr. Smithers. "What are you doing down there?" he asked in a stern voice.

6   I felt so ashamed of myself, I could hardly speak. Finally, I managed to explain why I was there and what I had suspected. I thought he would be furious with me, but he laughed until tears came to his eyes. I apologized to him for my mistake and he was nice enough to show me how he polished rocks.

    80

1   Based on the information in paragraph 1, Dr. Smithers is probably —

A   an old man
B   a medical doctor
C   a very wealthy man
D   a very popular person

2   The speaker in this story is probably —

A   a child
B   a father
C   an old man
D   a housekeeper

3   Why does the speaker think Dr. Smithers is building monsters?

A   The housekeeper told him that.
B   He hears strange noises coming from the basement.
C   He has just seen a movie about a doctor who builds a monster.
D   He saw a group of men carrying a monster into Dr. Smithers's house.

4   In paragraph 3, the word *aggravated* means —

A   angered
B   made worse
C   tired out
D   pleased

81

5 When the speaker told Dr. Smithers his suspicions, Dr. Smithers —

A was angry
B thought it was funny
C went into his laboratory
D told the speaker to go home

6 What lesson do you think the speaker learned from this experience?

A Don't trespass.
B Never trust a stranger.
C Be friendly to your neighbors.
D Don't rely on first impressions.

7 Why do you think the speaker thought Mildred was strange? Why do you think he mentions it?

_____

_____

_____

_____

_____

_____

_____

8 What do you think would have happened if Dr. Smithers had been willing and able to talk to the speaker when he or she came calling?

_____

_____

_____

_____

_____

_____

_____

8A Which of the following passages supports the answer you provided to the question above?

A Dr. Smithers had a strange housekeeper named Mildred. Mildred dressed in black and spoke with a foreign accent. One day, I went to Dr. Smithers's house. I was determined to find out what went on in the basement. Mildred would not let me in.

B I decided that I would sneak into Dr. Smithers's basement to find out what he did there. I waited for a night when Dr. Smithers was not working in the basement. One night, I saw that the basement lights were out.

C I stood in Dr. Smithers's basement, feeling embarrassed that I had suspected him of creating Frankenstein monsters. I heard the sound of a cane at the top of the basement stairs. I knew it was Dr. Smithers. "What are you doing down there?" he asked in a stern voice.

D I felt so ashamed of myself, I could hardly speak. Finally, I managed to explain why I was there and what I had suspected. I thought he would be furious with me, but he laughed until tears came to his eyes. I apologized to him for my mistake and he was nice enough to show me how he polished rocks.

WEBPAGE: TSUNAMI

RETURN TO YOUR SAFETY MAIN PAGE

Tsunami

Here at home, most Americans were nearing the end of their holiday celebrations and getting ready to welcome in the new year of 2005. On the other side of the globe, off the western coast of Indonesia, the ground suddenly shook. It had been hit with one of the most powerful earthquakes ever measured — 9.0 on the Richter scale. Because this tremendously strong earthquake happened deep in the Indian Ocean, it generated a powerful sea wave called a tsunami and led to one of the deadliest natural disasters in modern history.

Waves of up to 50 feet high hit more than 11 countries in Asia and Africa, many of them thousands of miles away from the earthquake. More than 200,000 people died as a result. Many drowned, and others were killed when buildings and other structures collapsed after being hit by the waves of water. But the problems didn't end with the tsunami itself. Survivers faced a big risk of infectious disease for three reasons: so many people were killed; basic electric, water and sewage services were destroyed; and food and water supplies were polluted.

Let's take a look at what tsunamis are and how they can affect the health of so many people directly in the path of the tsunami.

BAM! Home | Privacy Policy | Contact Us | About BAM! | Site Map

Source: Centers for Disease Control and Prevention, BAM! (www.bam.gov)]

1   What is a tsunami?

    A   A flood
    B   A holiday
    C   A strong wave
    D   An earthquake

2   What causes a tsunami?

    A   A flood
    B   A storm
    C   High tide
    D   An earthquake

3   According to the author, what is one reason the tsunami survivors risked getting sick?

    A   People drowned.
    B   There were earthquakes.
    C   Buildings were destroyed.
    D   Sewage systems stopped working.

4   To learn more about tsunamis, what link would you click on?

    A   What?
    B   Health issues?
    C   Where?
    D   In your area?

5   What section of the BAM! Web site is this page a part of?

    A   Diseases
    B   Food & nutrition
    C   Physical activity
    D   Your safety

THE STORY WITHOUT AN END

1   There was once a king who was very fond of stories. He lived a long time ago before there were any story-books.

2   So this king had people tell him stories. He could never hear enough. He would listen to his storytellers from morning until night.

3   The king was always sorry when a story came to an end. Another must be begun at once. Sometimes, though, no one was ready with a new story. Then the king became very angry.

4   At last he said: "Whoever will tell me a story that has no ending shall marry my daughter. And he shall be king after me. But whoever starts a story and ends it, him will I throw into prison. And there he shall stay."

5   Now the princess was very beautiful, and the kingdom was rich. So young princes and noblemen came from far and near with their stories.

6   The first one to come began his tale. He talked all day. The second and the third day he talked on and on. On the fourth day he could think of no more. He stammered and stopped. "Is that all?" asked the king. "Go on." But the young man could not say another word. "Away with him to the prison!" cried the king. "Next!"

7   Another began a story without a moment's delay. He talked and he talked day after day, and week after week. At last he, too, could say no more. And he was hurried away to prison.

8   This one was followed by a third. The third was followed by a fourth. And these were followed by many others. Some talked for weeks; some talked for months. All came to the end at last, and were thrown into prison.

9   So for a long time the story-loving king was quite happy. Though each storyteller had stopped at last, another was always ready to begin a new tale. Each one was sure he would win the princess and the kingdom. No one seemed to give a thought to the prison.

10   However, there came a day when no one appeared as the king cried, "Next!"

11   The king waited a whole day, two days, three days, a week. No one came with a story.

86

12   The king was getting impatient. He must have a story. At last he was about to free his prisoners and give each another chance, when a young man appeared before him. He was not a prince. He was not a nobleman. He was the son of a poor workman who lived near the palace.

13   "Well, what do you want?" asked the king, who knew the young man.

14   "I came to tell you a story," was the reply, "a story without an end."

15   "Indeed," sneered the king, "do you think you can do what a score of princes and noblemen have tried and given up?"

16   "I am ready to try," answered the young man.

17   "Begin, then, at once," said the king. "Only remember, when you stop, to prison you go."

18   "I have one favor to ask," said the youth.

19   "What is it?" asked the king, impatiently.

20   "Do you promise to listen to the end?"

21   "Yes, yes," cried the king; "only begin!"

22   The young man began.

23   "There was once a king who built a barn. It was the largest barn ever seen. It took hours to walk from one side of it to the other. It took weeks to walk the length of it.

24   Then the king had all his people sow all his lands with wheat. For miles and miles, there was nothing but wheat, wheat, wheat.

25   When the grain was ripe, the king had it all gathered into his great barn. But the barn was not full. Year after year the king's people sowed wheat. And all the ripe grain was gathered into this great barn. At last the king died, but still his barn was not full.

26   The king's son became king, and he made all the people sow wheat. And all the ripe grain was gathered into the king's great barn.

27   After many years the son died, and still the barn was not full. So one king followed another. And every one made all the people sow wheat. And all the ripe grain was gathered into the king's barn.

     87

28   At last, in the reign of the tenth king the great barn was filled full! Then the king had every door and every window closed tight."

29   "'Never before was there such a pile of wheat in the whole world,' cried the king. 'And it's all mine. And it's all safe. There's not the smallest hole or crack in that barn!'

30   But this proud king was wrong. There was just one hole in one corner of the barn. This hole was barely big enough to stick a large pin-head through. But this was enough!

31   One day a hungry ant came that way. He found the one hole into the barn. It was just big enough for him to crawl through. He went in and brought out a grain of wheat. When he came out, another ant went in and brought out a grain of wheat. And when this ant came out, another ant went in and brought out a grain of wheat. Then another ant went in and brought out a grain of wheat.

32   Then another ant went in and brought out a grain of wheat."

33   All day long the storyteller kept on saying, "Then another ant went in and brought out a grain of wheat."

34   In the morning the young man began again, "Then another ant went in and brought out a grain of wheat."

35   "All the ants must have been in and brought out a grain of wheat; on with the story," cried the king.

36   "No, no," answered the young man, "there was a whole big hill of them."

37   And he went on as before, "Then another ant went in and brought out a grain of wheat.

38   "Then another ant went in and brought out a grain of wheat."

39   So he kept on with the story day after day.

40   At last the king broke in again. "Surely," he cried, "every one of those ants has been into the barn and brought out a grain of wheat."

41   "True," answered the young man, "and now they are going in again, one at a time."

88

42   And he went on, "Then another ant went in and brought out a grain of wheat."

43   Week after week he kept up his story with these words, over and over, "Then another ant went in and brought out a grain of wheat."

44   At last the weary king interrupted again. "Ants don't live long," said he. "Every one of that hill of ants must have died long ago."

45   "True," answered the young man, with a smile, "the first hill of ants are all dead. It is their children that are going into the barn now. And after these have carried off grain all their lives, their children will take their places, and so on. Then another ant went—"

46   "Hold," cried the king, "leave that out, and go on with the story."

47   "No, king," answered the young man, "that is part of the story. I cannot omit it. And you have promised to listen to me."

48   So he went on again, "Then another ant went in and brought out a grain of wheat.

49   "Then another ant went in and brought out a grain of wheat."

50   And the king listened, month after month. Finally he could bear it no longer.

51   "Stop!" he cried. "Not another word! Take my daughter, take my kingdom, take everything I have! But never say ant or wheat to me again!"

52   So the young man was forced to end his story. The first thing he did was to set free the prisoners—the princes and noblemen who could not tell a story without an end. Then he married the beautiful princess. However, he would not take the kingdom until the king died.

1   Why did the king want someone to tell a story with no ending?

    A   In order to fill his prison
    B   Because it would help him sleep
    C   To find a husband for his daughter
    D   So he wouldn't have to keep looking for new storytellers

2   The young men who came to tell the king stories ended up in prison. Still, others came to tell him more stories. Why?

    A   They liked telling stories.
    B   They wanted to marry his daughter.
    C   They wanted to make their king happy.
    D   He was paying them a lot of money to tell stories

3   The young man who told a story with no end was —

    A   poor
    B   a prince
    C   a nobleman
    D   the king's son

4   In the story, how long did it probably take to fill the barn with wheat?

    A   A year
    B   Ten years
    C   Fifty years
    D   Hundreds of years

90

5 Why did the king keep interrupting the story of the barn?

   A He wanted to guess what happened next.
   B He wanted to know more about the lives of ants.
   C He got bored with the young man repeating the same sentence.
   D He did not want the young man to marry his daughter and become king.

6 The young man —

   A was a bad storyteller
   B was very anxious to become king
   C probably planned his story before going to the king
   D was coming to the end of the story when the king stopped him

7 Why did the king stop the young man's storytelling?

   A In order to send him to prison
   B Because he wanted to go to sleep
   C Because he wanted to bring in another storyteller
   D Because the constat repetition of the same sentence over and over again
      was driving him crazy.

91

7A Which of the following passages supports the answer you provided to the question above?

A   After many years the son died, and still the barn was not full. So one king followed another. And every one made all the people sow wheat. And all the ripe grain was gathered into the king's barn.

B   At last, in the reign of the tenth king the great barn was filled full! Then the king had every door and every window closed tight.

C   One day a hungry ant came that way. He found the one hole into the barn. It was just big enough for him to crawl through. He went in and brought out a grain of wheat. When he came out, another ant went in and brought out a grain of wheat. And when this ant came out, another ant went in and brought out a grain of wheat. Then another ant went in and brought out a grain of wheat.

D   Stop!" he cried. "Not another word! Take my daughter, take my kingdom, take everything I have! But never say ant or wheat to me again!"

8   If you were the young man, which would be more important to you, marrying the princess or becoming king someday?

_____

_____

_____

_____

_____

_____

_____

_____

_____

_____

IF EVER I SEE

by Lydia Maria Child

1   If ever I see,
2   On bush or tree,
3   Young birds in their pretty nest,
4   I must not in play
5   Steal the birds away
6   To grieve their mother's breast.
7   My mother, I know,
8   Would sorrow so,
9   Should I be stolen away;
10   So I'll speak to the birds
11   In my softest words,
12 Nor hurt them in my play.
13   And when they can fly
14   In the bright blue sky,
15 They'll warble a song to me;
16   And then if I'm sad,
17   It will make me glad
18 To think they are happy and free.

LITTLE CHILDREN, NEVER GIVE

1   Little children, never give
2   Pain to things that feel and live.
3   Let the gentle robin come
4   For the crumbs you save at home.
5   As his feed you throw along
6   He'll repay you with a song.
7   Never hurt the timid hare
8   Peeping from her green grass lair.
9   Let her come and sport and play
10 On the lawn at close of day.
11 The little lark goes soaring high
12 To the bright windows of the sky,
13 Singing as if 'twere always spring
14 And fluttering on an untired wing.
15 Oh! let him sing his happy song,
16 Nor do these gentle creatures wrong.

1   What is the message of both poems?

    A   Animals will not hurt you.
    B   You shouldn't hurt animals.
    C   Children enjoy feeding birds.
    D   There are animals all around us.

2   In the first poem, why won't the speaker take young birds from their nest?

    A   She can't reach the nest.
    B   The birds are singing to her.
    C   The mother bird chases her away.
    D   She doesn't want the mother bird to be sad.

3   The speaker in the first poem is —

    A   a child
    B   a parent
    C   a teacher
    D   the author

4   The animals in the second poem probably visit a —

    A   shopping center
    B   parking lot
    C   garden
    D   school

5   The two poems differ in —

    A   the number of verses
    B   their rhyme patterns
    C   their themes
    D   no way at all

94

LIFE AS A WILDLIFE BIOLOGIST

by Genny Fannucchi

Adapted from: EEK! – Environmental Education for Kids! Wisconsin Department of Natural Resources (dnr.wi.gov/eek/).

1   Life as a wildlife biologist is interesting. You never know what's around the corner. You also never know what kind of skills you'll need to build your career. That's why it's a good idea to keep an open mind and try a lot of things.

2   A wildlife biologist needs to have different kinds of skills and education. School is important, and an interest in biology and science is handy. It's a good idea to go to college to get a degree in wildlife ecology or some related field.

3   Every day is different. One day, you might be doing an eagle survey. The next day, you might be mending a fence on your property. A day later, you could be conducting a burn to restore prairies. That evening, you might be giving a safety course for hunters or holding a turkey education clinic. One thing is for sure—you'll spend time outside observing nature and improving the land for wildlife.

4   Even though it's a lot of work, it's fun. You'll be tired at night—but happy!

1   The author probably thinks that a job as a wildlife biologist —

A   can be boring
B   is too dangerous
C   has a lot of variety
D   means spending too much time at your desk

2   In paragraph 2, what does field mean?

A   Countryside
B   Entertain
C   Meadow
D   Subject

3   Paragraph 3 —

    A   defines the word biologist
    B   gives examples of what wildlife biologists do
    C   tells what a wildlife biologist does in a usual day
    D   gives reasons why being a wildlife biologist is fun

from ALICE IN WONDERLAND

by Alice Gerstenberg

SCENE THREE

When the curtain rises, one sees nothing but odd black lanterns with orange lights, hanging from the sky. The lights come up slowly, revealing Alice seated on two large cushions. She has been left there by the White Queen and is dazed to find herself in a strange hall with many peculiar doors and knobs that are too high to reach.

Alice: Oh! my head! Where am I? Oh dear, Oh dear! *(She staggers up and to her amazement finds herself smaller than the table.)* I've never been smaller than any table before! I've always been able to reach the knobs! What a curious feeling. Oh! I'm shrinking. It's the fan and the gloves! *(She throws them away, feels her head, and measures herself against table and doors.)* Oh! saved in time! But I never …

White Rabbit: Oh! my fan and gloves! Where are my …

Alice: Oh! Mr. Rabbit, please help me out! I want to go home! I want to go home!

White Rabbit: Oh! the Duchess! Oh! my fur and whiskers! She'll get me executed, as sure as ferrets are ferrets! Oh! you have them!

Alice: I'm sorry. You dropped them, you know.

White Rabbit: *(Picking up fan and gloves and pattering off)* She'll chop off your head!

Alice: If you please, sir—where am I? Won't you please tell me how to get out? I want to get out!

White Rabbit: *(Looking at his watch)* Oh! my ears and whiskers, how late it's getting. *(A trap door gives way and Rabbit disappears. Alice dashes after him just in time to have the trap door bang in her face.)*

Alice: *(Amazed)* It's a rabbit-hole. I'm small enough to fit into it, too! If I shrink any more, I might go out altogether like a candle. I wonder what I would look like then. What does the flame of a candle look like after the candle is blown out? I've never seen such a thing.

Humpty Dumpty: *(Sitting on wall)* Don't stand chattering to yourself like that. Tell me your name and your business.

97

Alice: My name is Alice, but …

Humpty Dumpty: That's a stupid name. What does it mean?

Alice: Must a name mean something?

Humpty Dumpty: Of course it must; my name means the shape I am—and a good, handsome shape it is, too. With a name like yours, you might be almost any shape.

Alice: You're Humpty Dumpty! Just like an egg.

Humpty Dumpty: It's very provoking, to be called an egg—very.

Alice: I said you looked like an egg, Sir, and some eggs are very pretty, you know.

Humpty Dumpty: Some people have no more sense than a baby.

Alice: Why do you sit here all alone?

Humpty Dumpty: Why, because there's nobody with me. Did you think I didn't know the answer to that? Ask another.

Alice: Don't you think you'd be safer down on the ground? That wall's so very narrow.

Humpty Dumpty: What tremendously easy riddles you ask! Of course I don't think so. Take a good look at me! I'm one that has spoken to a king, I am. To show you I'm not proud, you may shake hands with me! *(He leans forward to offer Alice his hand but she is too small to reach it.)* However, this conversation is going on a little too fast. Let's go back to the last remark but one.

Alice: I'm afraid I can't remember it.

Humpty Dumpty: In that case, we'll start fresh. It's my turn to choose a subject.

Alice: You talk about it as if it were a game.

Humpty Dumpty: So here's a question for you. How old did you say you were?

Alice: Seven years and six months.

Humpty Dumpty: Wrong! You never said a word about it. Now, if you'd asked my advice, I'd have said, "Leave off at seven, but ... "

Alice: I never ask advice about growing.

Humpty Dumpty: Too proud?

Alice: What a beautiful belt you've got on. At least, a beautiful cravat, I should have said. No, a belt, I mean. I beg your pardon. If only I knew which was neck and which was waist!

Humpty Dumpty: It is a most provoking thing, when a person doesn't know a cravat from a belt.

Alice: I know. It's very ignorant of me.

Humpty Dumpty: It's a cravat, child, and a beautiful one, as you say. There's glory for you.

Alice: I don't know what you mean by "glory."

Humpty Dumpty: When I use a word, it means just what I choose it to mean—neither more nor less.

Alice: The question is—can you make words mean different things?

Humpty Dumpty: The question is—which is to be master? That's all. Impenetrability! That's what I say!

Alice: Would you tell me, please, what that means?

Humpty Dumpty: I meant by "impenetrability" that we've had enough of that subject, and it would be just as well if you'd mention what you mean to do next, as I suppose you don't mean to stop here all the rest of your life.

Alice: That's a great deal to make one word mean.

Humpty Dumpty: When I make a word do a lot of work like that, I always pay it extra.

Alice: Oh!

Humpty Dumpty: Ah, you should see them come to me on a Saturday night—to get their wages, you know. That's all. Good-bye.

Alice: Good-bye, till we meet again.

Humpty Dumpty: I shouldn't know you again if we did meet. You're so exactly like other people.

Alice: The face is what one goes by, generally.

Humpty Dumpty: That's just what I complain of. Your face is the same as everybody else's—two eyes, nose in the middle, mouth under it. It's always the same. Now, if you had the two eyes on the same side of the nose, for instance— or the mouth at the top—that would be of some help.

Alice: It wouldn't look nice.

Humpty Dumpty: Wait till you've tried! Good-bye. (He disappears as he came.)

1 At the beginning of the scene, why is Alice upset?

   A   The White Queen has hit her.
   B   The White Rabbit has lost his hat.
   C   She finds that she is growing smaller.
   D   Humpty-Dumpty has fallen down and broken.

2 Some parts of the text are in parentheses. Why?

   A   These words give the thoughts of the characters.
   B   These are the words the characters speak.
   C   These parts explain the time and setting.
   D   They describe the characters' actions.

3 The White Rabbit probably —

   A   is getting dressed
   B   does not care about Alice
   C   goes to look for Humpty Dumpty
   D   does not care what the Duchess thinks

100

4   From the reading, which of the following is true?

    A   Alice is worried that Humpty-Dumpty might fall.
    B   Alice has met Humpty-Dumpty before.
    C   Humpty-Dumpty thinks Alice is special.
    D   Humpty-Dumpty likes Alice's cravat.

5   Which word best describes Humpty Dumpty?

    A   Gloomy
    B   Round
    C   Shy
    D   Skinny

6   Humpty-Dumpty says he won't recognize Alice next time they meet. What reason does he give?

    A   She looks like everyone else.
    B   He has a very bad memory.
    C   He has never seen her before.
    D   She will be taller than she is now.

7   Humpty-Dumpty seems to think that because he has spoken to someone important, he won't fall from where he is sitting. To whom did he speak who was so important?

    A   The king
    B   The Duchess
    C   The White Rabbit
    D   Alice

101

7A Which of the following passages supports the answer you provided to the question above?

    A White Rabbit: Oh! the Duchess! Oh! my fur and whiskers! She'll get me executed, as sure as ferrets are ferrets! Oh! you have them!

    B Humpty Dumpty: When I use a word, it means just what I choose it to mean—neither more nor less.

    C Humpty Dumpty: When I make a word do a lot of work like that, I always pay it extra.

    D Humpty Dumpty: What tremendously easy riddles you ask! Of course I don't think so. Take a good look at me! I'm one that has spoken to a king, I am. To show you I'm not proud, you may shake hands with me! (He leans forward to offer Alice his hand but she is too small to reach it.) However, this conversation is going on a little too fast. Let's go back to the last remark but one.

8   Do you think you would have a hard time understanding Humpty Dumpty if you had a conversation with him? Why or why not?

_____

_____

_____

_____

_____

_____

_____

_____

_____

TWO READINGS ABOUT A ZOO

READING ONE:
INTERVIEW WITH JUAN RODRIGUEZ

Adapted from: Career Spotlight, Kids.gov.

Career: Animal Keeper
Date: September 28, 2010
Place: The National Zoo, Washington D.C.

1   My name is Juan Rodriguez. I'm an animal keeper at the National Zoo.

2   I first I realized I loved animals when my older brother brought home injured pigeons and stray cats and dogs. I fell in love with taking care of animals. I was seven years old.

3   My love of working with animals was the main reason I got involved at the National Zoo. Becoming a volunteer was the first stepping stone to becoming a full-time employee. They told me what my responsibilities were and what I needed to do to become a keeper. After I was a volunteer for several months, I was able to get a job here. I didn't have a college degree when I first started back in 1997, but later I got my degree in biology.

4   What do we do day to day? When we arrive in the morning, we make sure the animals aren't sick and everything's normal. We get a head count of all the animals we're in charge of. Then, if any of them need medication, we give it to them. After that, we do a lot of things, such as research, behavioral watches, and cleaning stalls. You've got to do the dirty work, too! We also talk to the public about the sloth bears and all the other animals in the Nature Trail and explain what they can do about conservation.

5   I think my favorite part of the job is when I'm talking to the public and they learn something new about an animal that I work with. You can just see a light bulb flash in their heads. You know they're thinking, "Wow, this is something really amazing! I didn't know that about this animal."

6   My second favorite thing is when the animals are actually enjoying an enrichment item we have put in the yard for them. Enrichment items are toys and food treats we use to help re-create an animal's natural habitat. They encourage animals to play, learn, and grow. For example, we give the sloth bears some big balls. We drill holes in the balls and put the bears' kibble into them. The bears will roll them around for minutes or even hours to try to get the food out.

103

7   I think the best advice I have for kids is this: If you love working with animals, just follow your passion. If you're really determined, you'll find a way to succeed.

READING TWO:
THE NATIONAL ZOOLOGICAL PARK

1   The National Zoological Park is in Washington, D.C. It is run by the Smithsonian.

2   The National Zoo—another name for the Park—is very old. It opened more than 120 years ago. At that time, the Smithsonian was already collecting animals. It kept its animals in cages behind its buildings. When the zoo opened, it moved the animals into the new zoo.

3   From the beginning, the zoo housed its animals in open, park-like areas. The park began in a piece of land along Rock Creek. It was designed by a famous landscape designer, Frederick Law Olmstead. He made pastures where animals could graze and rocky areas where they could climb.

4   Like the Smithsonian, the zoo's main purpose was education. From the beginning, it brought in rare and endangered species. As the United States grew, people took over more and more land. Many animals lost their homes. These animals were brought to the zoo. Since then, the U.S. government and even foreign countries have given animals to the zoo. Today, it has more than 500 different types of animals, including a white Bengal tiger and a pair of pandas.

5   The zoo continues to grow. Recently, it opened a Cheetah Conservation Station and a Reptile Discovery Center. It also built a rainforest, with the animals and plants that live in it. All these things help people preserve and learn more about animals.

1   Which of these is a difference between the two readings?

A   They are about different zoos.
B   One talks about the animals in the zoo, and the other does not.
C   One mentions education at the zoo, the other does not.
D   The author of the first is telling about his own experiences, while the author of the second is not.

2   When did Juan Rodriguez learn that he loved taking care of animals?

    A   As a child
    B   The first time he visited a zoo
    C   When he was studying biology
    D   When he started working at the zoo

3   One main goal of the National Zoo is —

    A   educating its animal keepers
    B   cleaning up the environment
    C   preserving the rainforest
    D   educating the public

4   The National Zoo —

    A   opened in the 1990s
    B   is not open to the public
    C   has only volunteer animal keepers
    D   helps preserve endangered animals

5   At the National Zoo, animals —

    A   live in cages
    B   all take medication
    C   live in their natural habitats
    D   are all from the American wilderness

6   Read the third paragraph in the second reading again. What does a landscape designer probably do?

    A   Build zoos
    B   Run a farm
    C   Work with animals
    D   Plan how park-like areas should look

WEBPAGE: COLONIAL AMERICA

★Home ★About this site ★Help ★Search   ★The Library of Congress

America's Story from America's Library

Meet Amazing Americans | Jump Back in Time | Explore the States | Join America at Play | See, Hear and Sing

Jump Back in Time ▸ Colonial America (1492-1763)

Columbus Reaches the Americas	"America" First Used	Magellan Circles the Globe	Cabrillo Explores California Coast	Spain Founds Colony in Florida	English Navy Defeats Armada
1480	1500	1520	1540	1560	1580

COLONIAL AMERICA

The Pilgrims landing on Plymouth Rock, December 1620

Click for enlargement and credits

European nations came to the Americas to increase their wealth and broaden their influence over world affairs. The Spanish were among the first Europeans to explore the New World and the first to settle in what is now the United States.

By 1650, however, England had established a dominant presence on the Atlantic coast. The first colony was founded at Jamestown, Virginia, in 1607. Many of the people who settled in the New World came to escape religious persecution. The Pilgrims, founders of Plymouth, Massachusetts, arrived in 1620. In both Virginia and Massachusetts, the colonists flourished with some assistance from Native Americans. New World grains such as corn kept the colonists from starving while, in Virginia, tobacco provided a valuable cash crop. By the early 1700s enslaved Africans made up a growing percentage of the colonial population. By 1770, more than 2 million people lived and worked in Great Britain's 13 North American colonies.

○ Freedom in Rhode Island

○ A Settlement with Unsettling Challenges

MORE STORIES

Source: America's Story, America's Library, Library of Congress
(www.americaslibrary.gov)]

1 When did the Pilgrims land at Plymouth Rock?

   A 1607
   B 1620
   C 1650
   D 1770

2 Where did England set up its first colony in North America?

   A California
   B Massachusetts
   C Rhode Island
   D Virginia

3 Tobacco was important to the English colonies because —

   A it kept the colonists from starving
   B the colonists could sell it for money
   C it increased the health of the colonists
   D Native Americans could sell it to colonists

4 The time line above the text —

   A lets you read other stories about colonial America
   B tells you about the history of Spanish exploration
   C shows when this story occurred in U.S. history
   D is not related to the text on this Web page

5   What link would you click to read about interesting people in U.S. history?

   A   Meet Amazing Americans
   B   Explore the States
   C   Join America at Play
   D   See, Hear and Sing

6   A good title for the text on this page would be —

   A   Colonial America
   B   The Pilgrims and Plymouth Colony
   C   English Settlement in North America
   D   European Exploration of the Americas

108

AN UNLIKELY HERO

1   In 1913, an unlikely hero was born. Her name was Rosa McCauley. Rosa was born in Alabama. When she was a child, her parents separated, and she grew up with her mother and grandmother in Montgomery. As a teenager, Rosa dropped out of high school to take care of her grandmother. At 19, Rosa married a barber named Raymond Parks. He encouraged her to go back to school and get her high school diploma. She later became a seamstress.

2   In Alabama, life could be hard for African Americans like Rosa and Raymond Parks. One reason for this was the Jim Crow laws. These laws kept the races separate, or segregated. There were different schools for whites and for "persons of color." There were different theaters and restaurants—and even different parks and cemeteries. African Americans were not allowed to use elevators. They always had to walk up the stairs. They were not allowed to sit at the front of a bus—even if the seats were empty. Also, if African Americans found seats in the middle of the bus and the "white seats" at the front were full, they had to give up their seats to any white passengers who boarded after them.

3   On December 1, 1955, after a long day at work, Rosa Parks found herself in just that situation. The back of the bus was full, and she took a seat in the middle. A few stops later, a white man got on the bus and wanted a seat. The driver told the people in the middle section to get up and make room for him. Three others stood up, but Rosa did not. The driver stopped the bus and called the police. The police arrested Rosa.

4   That day, Rosa started the movement that would end the Jim Crow laws. People across the South followed her lead. They began to protest segregation. People held sit-ins, eat-ins, and other protests. In Montgomery, they refused to ride the city buses for over a year. Finally, the order came to <u>desegregate</u> them.

5   Rosa Parks received many awards. Among them were the Presidential Medal of Freedom and the Congressional Gold Medal. Today, we remember her as the mother of the Civil Rights Movement.

1   What laws made African Americans go to different schools than white
    Americans?

    A   African laws
    B   Civil Rights laws
    C   Jim Crow laws
    D   Separation laws

2   Why is Rosa Parks called "the mother of the Civil Rights Movement"?

    A   Her action began the protest movement.
    B   Her children were leaders of the movement.
    C   She was born just before the movement began.
    D   She worked with other civil rights leaders to plan protest actions.

3   Which of these statements about Rosa Parks is not true?

    A   She dropped out of high school.
    B   She later earned a college degree.
    C   She received the Presidential Medal of Freedom.
    D   She refused to give up her seat to a white bus passenger.

4   Look at the word *desegregate* in paragraph 4. What does the "*de–*" at the
    beginning of the word mean?

    A   After
    B   Bad
    C   From
    D   Not

110

5   In paragraph 2, why does the writer talk about the Jim Crow laws?

   A   To explain why Rosa Parks dropped out of school
   B   Because these laws went against people's civil rights
   C   So that readers will understand the different types of protests
   D   To show how difficult life was for African Americans in the South

6   Read paragraph 4 again. That paragraph —

   A   tells a story
   B   compares Rosa and other protesters
   C   discusses how Rosa's actions caused other protests
   D   explains Rosa's reasons for not giving up her bus seat

7   Why did Rosa drop out of school?

   A   To take care of her grandmother.
   B   To become a seamstress..
   C   Her husband encouraged her to.
   D   The Jim Crow laws forced her to.

7A   Which of the following passages supports the answer you provided to the question above?

    A   In Alabama, life could be hard for African Americans like Rosa and Raymond Parks. One reason for this was the Jim Crow laws. These laws kept the races separate, or segregated. There were different schools for whites and for "persons of color."

    B   African Americans were not allowed to use elevators. They always had to walk up the stairs. They were not allowed to sit at the front of a bus—even if the seats were empty. Also, if African Americans found seats in the middle of the bus and the "white seats" at the front were full, they had to give up their seats to any white passengers who boarded after them.

    C   When she was a child, her parents separated, and she grew up with her mother and grandmother in Montgomery. As a teenager, Rosa dropped out of high school to take care of her grandmother.

    D   At 19, Rosa married a barber named Raymond Parks. He encouraged her to go back to school and get her high school diploma. She later became a seamstress.

8   How did Rosa Park's action lead directly to desegregation of the buses in Montgomery?

_____

_____

_____

_____

_____

_____

_____

_____

_____

CETACEANS

Adapted from: *National Oceanic & Atmospheric Administration (NOAA), U.S. Department of Commerce, http://www.noaa.gov.*

1   Whales, dolphins, and porpoises fascinate many people. This may be because of their size or their playful actions. It may result from the attention that has been focused on human threats to them. These creatures of the sea are mammals, just like humans. They breathe air. They are warm-blooded. They bear live young called calves, which are nursed by their mothers.

2   There are seven species of cetaceans in U.S. waters that are protected under the Endangered Species Act. They are the blue whale, the bowhead whale, the fin whale, the humpback whale, the northern light whale, the sei whale, and the sperm whale. All seven species are listed as endangered.

SPECIES OF CETACEANS IN U.S. WATERS PROTECTED UNDER THE SEA	
Species	**Where they are found**
Blue Whale	All oceans
Bowhead Whale	Arctic seas
Fin Whale	All oceans
Humpback Whale	Along coasts in all oceans
Right Whale	North Atlantic, North Pacific
Sei Whale	All oceans
Sperm Whale	Warm waters

113

3   How did these whales become endangered? People hunted and killed so many of them that their numbers were greatly reduced. During the 19th century, whales were hunted primarily for oil and baleen. Before we had electricity, many Americans used whale oil to light their homes. Baleen was used in fans and corsets. Not long ago, products from whales were still used for everything from machine oil to women's cosmetics. However, in 1972, it became illegal to import products containing materials from whales.

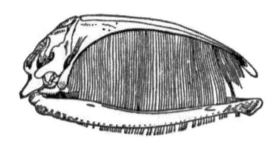

Baleen, or whalebone, is a sort of sieve in some whales' mouths that separates food from water.

4   Two whale species show what may happen in the future. Both the gray whale and the right whale were hunted almost to extinction. The gray whale may be a symbol of hope. Their numbers have risen, and the gray whale has been removed from the endangered species list. In contrast, there are fewer than 400 right whales even though no one has hunted them for over 50 years,. It may take 100 years more for right whales to recover. Humans are still a problem for the slow-moving right whale; one of the major causes of death for them is collisions with ships.

1   What are cetaceans?

   A   Mammals
   B   A type of fish
   C   Endangered animals
   D   Whales, dolphins, and porpoises

2   Whales are different from humans because they —

   A   breathe air
   B   live in the sea
   C   are mammals
   D   are warm-blooded

114

3   Why were whales hunted?

   A   For sport
   B   For many useful products
   C   To keep their population down
   D   To protect other animals from them

4   The drawing —

   A   shows what whales look like
   B   depicts how baleen can be used
   C   explains why people hunted whales
   D   helps readers understand what baleen is

5   Based on the information in the table, which of these statements is true?

   A   Whales can be found all over the world.
   B   Blue whales stay mostly in warm waters.
   C   Gray whales are on the endangered species list.
   D   Humpback whales avoid areas where there are a lot of people.

6   Paragraph 4 —

   A   gives a history of whale hunting
   B   contrasts the situations of two whale species
   C   gives examples of different types of cetaceans
   D   explains the ways in which humans endanger whales

115

WEBPAGE: WATER TREATMENT PROCESS

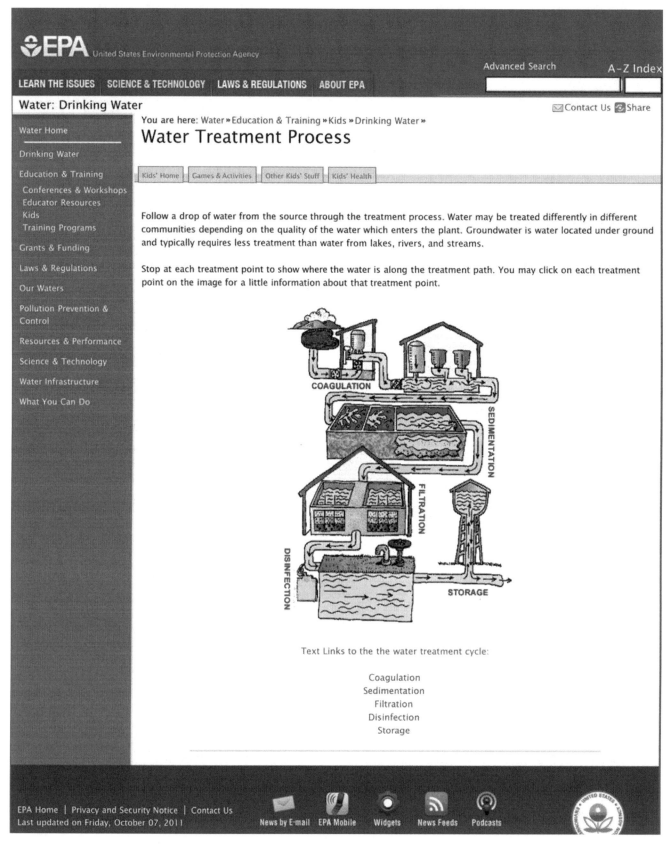

Source: United States Environmental Protection Agency, http://water.epa.gov

1 Water is treated —

A before sending it to lakes, rivers, and streams
B when it comes from groundwater
C to create clean drinking water
D after we use it

2 What is the last step in the water treatment process?

A Coagulation
B Disinfection
C Filtration
D Sedimentation

3 The diagram on this page shows —

A the water treatment process
B how water is filtered
C where water is stored
D why water quality is not always the same

4 Groundwater comes from

A Lakes
B Storage tanks
C Under the ground
D Water treatment plants

5 Why is water treated differently in different communities?

A Water quality is not the same everywhere.
B Some communities cannot afford to treat their water.
C Some people do not like the taste of treated water.
D Each part of the plant uses a different process.

117

from FIGHTING THE WHALES

by R. M. Ballantyne

1   I shall never forget the surprise I got the first time I saw a whale.

2   It was in the forenoon of a most splendid day, about a week after we arrived at that part of the ocean where we might expect to find fish. A light northeast breeze was blowing, but it scarcely ruffled the sea, as we crept slowly through the water with every stitch of canvas set.

3   As we had been looking out for fish for some time past, everything was in readiness for them. The boats were hanging over the side ready to lower, tubs for coiling away the ropes, harpoons, lances, etc., all were ready to throw in and start away at a moment's notice. The man in the crow's nest, as they call the cask fixed up at the masthead, was looking anxiously out for whales, and the crew were idling about the deck. Tom Lokins was seated on the windlass, smoking his pipe, and I was sitting beside him on an empty cask, sharpening a blubber-knife.

4   "Tom," said I, "what is like a whale?"

5   "Why, it's like nothing but itself," replied Tom, looking puzzled. "Why, what a queer fellow you are to ask questions."

6   "I'm sure you've seen plenty of them. You might be able to tell what a whale is like."

7   "What it's like! Well, it's like a tremendous big bolster with a head and a tail to it."

8   "And how big is it?"

9   "They're of all sizes, lad. I've seen one that was exactly equal to 300 fat bulls, and its <u>rate of going</u> would take it round the whole world in 23 days."

10   "I don't believe you," said I, laughing.

11   "Don't you?" cried Tom; "it's a fact notwithstanding, for the captain himself said so, and that's how I came to know it."

12   Just as Tom finished speaking, the man in the crow's nest roared at the top of his voice, "There she blows!"

13   That was the signal that a whale was in sight, and as it was the first time we had heard it that season, every man in the ship was thrown into a state of tremendous excitement.

14   "There she blows!" roared the man again.

15   "Where away?" shouted the captain.

16   "About two miles right ahead."

17   In another moment the utmost excitement prevailed on board. Suddenly, while I was looking over the side, straining my eyes to catch a sight of the whale, which could not yet be seen by the men on deck, I saw a brown object appear in the sea, not twenty yards from the side of the ship. Before I had time to ask what it was, a whale's head rose to the surface and shot up out of the water. The part of the fish that was visible above water could not have been less than thirty feet in length. It looked just as if our longboat had jumped out of the sea, and he was so near that I could see his great mouth quite plainly. I could have tossed a biscuit on his back easily. Sending two thick spouts of frothy water out of his blowholes forty feet into the air with tremendous noise, he fell flat upon the sea with a clap like thunder, tossed his <u>flukes</u>, or tail, high into the air, and disappeared.

18   I was so amazed at this sight that I could not speak. I could only stare at the place where the huge monster had gone down.

1   Where does this story take place?

A   In New England
B   On a whaling ship
C   On an ocean liner
D   In a lifeboat on the ocean

2   In paragraph 9, what does Tom mean by "rate of going"?

A   direction
B   speed
C   swimming
D   walking

3   When he sees a whale for the first time, the speaker —

    A   is afraid
    B   throws a harpoon
    C   is surprised by how big it is
    D   calls out, "There she blows!"

4   In this story, what does *flukes* (paragraph 17) mean?

    A   accidents
    B   chances
    C   good luck
    D   tail

5   Who has the best view of the sea?—

    A   the speaker
    B   Tom
    C   the man in the crow's nest
    D   the captain

5 A. Which of the following passages supports the answer you provided to the question above?

A   It was in the forenoon of a most splendid day, about a week after we arrived at that part of the ocean where we might expect to find fish. A light northeast breeze was blowing, but it scarcely ruffled the sea, as we crept slowly through the water with every stitch of canvas set.

B   As we had been looking out for fish for some time past, everything was in readiness for them. The boats were hanging over the side ready to lower, tubs for coiling away the ropes, harpoons, lances, etc., all were ready to throw in and start away at a moment's notice. The man in the crow's nest, as they call the cask fixed up at the masthead, was looking anxiously out for whales, and the crew were idling about the deck.

C   In another moment the utmost excitement prevailed on board. Suddenly, while I was looking over the side, straining my eyes to catch a sight of the whale, which could not yet be seen by the men on deck, I saw a brown object appear in the sea, not twenty yards from the side of the ship.

D   Before I had time to ask what it was, a whale's head rose to the surface and shot up out of the water. The part of the fish that was visible above water could not have been less than thirty feet in length.

6. Why did the man in the crow's nest yell, "There she blows" instead of "There she is?"

_____

_____

_____

_____

_____

_____

_____

_____

7. A whale is a mammal, not a fish. Why do you think the speaker calls it a fish?

_____

_____

_____

_____

_____

_____

_____

_____

_____

_____

_____

SHAKESPEARE'S KING LEAR
by E. Nesbit

1   King Lear was old and tired. He was weary of the business of his kingdom and wished only to end his days quietly near his three daughters. Two of his daughters were married to the Dukes of Albany and Cornwall; and the Duke of Burgundy and the King of France both wanted to marry Cordelia, his youngest daughter.

2   Lear called his three daughters together and told them that he proposed to divide his kingdom between them. "But first," said he, "I should like to know how much you love me."

3   Goneril, who was really a very wicked woman and did not love her father at all, said she loved him more than words could say; she loved him dearer than eyesight, space, or liberty, more than life, grace, health, beauty, and honor.

4   "I love you as much as my sister and more," professed Regan, "since I care for nothing but my father's love."

5   Lear was very much pleased with Regan's professions and turned to his youngest daughter, Cordelia. "Now, though last not least," he said, "the best part of my kingdom I have kept for you. What can you say?"

6   "Nothing, my lord," answered Cordelia.

7   "Nothing can come of nothing. Speak again," said the King.

8   And Cordelia answered, "I love your Majesty according to my duty—no more, no less." She said this because she was disgusted with the way in which her sisters professed love when they did not even feel a sense of duty to their old father.

9   "I am your daughter," she went on, "and you have brought me up and loved me, and I return you those duties back as are right and fit, obey you, love you, and most honor you."

10   Lear, who loved Cordelia best, had wished her to make more extravagant professions of love than her sisters. "Go," he said, "be forever a stranger to my heart and me."

11   The Earl of Kent, one of Lear's favorite courtiers and captains, tried to say a word for Cordelia's sake, but Lear would not listen. He divided the kingdom between Goneril and Regan, and told them that he should only keep a hundred knights at arms and would live with his daughters by turns.

123

12   When the Duke of Burgundy knew that Cordelia would have no share of the kingdom, he no longer wanted to marry her. But the King of France was wiser and said, "Thy dowerless daughter, King, is Queen of us—and our fair France."

13   "Take her, take her," said the King, "for I will never see that face of hers again."

14   So Cordelia became Queen of France, and the Earl of Kent, for taking her part, was banished from the kingdom. The King now went to stay with his daughter Goneril, who had everything from her father that he had to give and now began to grudge even the hundred knights he had reserved for himself. She showed him no respect, and her servants either refused to obey his orders or pretended that they did not hear them.

15   Now the Earl of Kent, when he was banished, pretended to go to another country, but instead he came back to the King in the disguise of a servant. The King now had two friends—the Earl of Kent, whom he only knew as his servant, and his Fool, who was faithful to him. Goneril told her father plainly that his knights only served to fill her Court with riot and feasting; so she begged him only to keep a few old men about him such as himself.

16   My train are men who know all parts of duty," said Lear. "Goneril, I will not trouble you further. I have another daughter." And his horses being saddled, he set out with his followers for Regan's castle. But Regan, who had formerly outdone her sister in professions of attachment to the King, now seemed to outdo her in harsh conduct, saying that fifty knights were too many to wait on him, and Goneril (who had hurried thither to prevent Regan showing any kindness to the old King) said five were too many, since Regan's servants could wait on him.

17   Lear saw that what they really wanted was to drive him away, and he left them. It was a wild and stormy night, and he wandered about the heath half mad with misery, and with no companion but the poor Fool. After a while, his servant, the good Earl of Kent, met him, and at last persuaded him to lie down in a wretched little hut. At daybreak, the Earl of Kent took his royal master to Dover and hurried to the Court of France to tell Cordelia what had happened.

18   Cordelia's husband gave her an army, and with it she landed at Dover. Here she found poor King Lear, wandering about the fields, wearing a crown of nettles and weeds. They brought him back to France and fed and clothed him. Cordelia came to him and kissed him.

124

19   "You must bear with me," said Lear. "Forget and forgive. I am old and foolish."
     And now, he knew at last which of his children it was that had loved him best
     and who was worthy of his love.

1   Which of King Lear's daughters did he love most?

    A   Cordelia
    B   Goneril
    C   Regan
    D   Kent

2   Why did Lear send Cordelia away?

    A   She did not love him.
    B   He wanted her to marry the King of France.
    C   She did not use fancy words to express her love.
    D   He did not love her as much as he did her sisters.

3   Why did Goneril and Regan tell their father how much they loved him?

    A   Because they wanted him to be happy
    B   So that he would give them his kingdom
    C   To convince him to come and live with them
    D   Because they felt it was their duty to love him

4   Who remained loyal to King Lear?

    A   Goneril and Regan
B   The Earl of Kent and the Fool
    C   The Duke of Burgundy
    D   His daughters' servants

125

5 What lesson did King Lear learn?

    A Actions speak louder than words.
    B Beauty is only skin deep.
    C You can't trust anyone.
    D Turn the other cheek.

126

THE GETTYSBURG ADDRESS

by Abraham Lincoln

1   Four score and seven years ago, our fathers brought forth upon this continent a new nation, conceived in liberty and dedicated to the proposition that all men are created equal.

2   Now, we are engaged in a great civil war, testing whether that nation, or any nation so conceived and so dedicated, can long endure. We are met on a great battlefield of that war.

3   We have come to dedicate a portion of that field as a final resting place for those who here gave their lives that this nation might live. It is altogether fitting and proper that we should do this.

4   But, in a larger sense, we cannot dedicate, we cannot consecrate, we cannot hallow this ground. The brave men, living and dead, who struggled here have consecrated it far above our poor power to add or detract. The world will little note, nor long remember, what we say here, but it can never forget what they did here.

5   It is for us, the living, rather, to be dedicated here to the unfinished work which they who fought here have thus far so nobly advanced. It is rather for us to be here dedicated to the great task remaining before us—that from these honored dead we take increased devotion to that cause for which they gave the last full measure of devotion; that we here highly resolve that these dead shall not have died in vain; that this nation, under God, shall have a new birth of freedom; and that government of the people, by the people, for the people shall not perish from this earth.

1   "The Gettysburg Address" is a speech given by President Abraham Lincoln. Where did he give the speech?

    A In a graveyard
    B On a battlefield
    C Before Congress
    D At the White House

2   Why have Lincoln and others come to that place?

   A To fight a battle in a civil war
   B To remember the founding fathers
   C To make speeches people will remember
   D To dedicate the land to those who died there

3   In paragraph 1, the nation Lincoln talks about is —

   A England
   B France
   C North America
   D the United States

4   In his speech, Lincoln says —

   A the country must forget the pain of battle
   B Americans must remember what he says that day
   C no one will remember those who died at Gettysburg
   D Americans must commit themselves to saving the nation

128

from THE PERFECT TRIBUTE

by Mary Raymond Shipman Andrews

1   At eleven o'clock in the morning of November 19, 1863, a silent crowd billowed like waves of the sea over what had been the battlefield of Gettysburg. There were wounded soldiers who, four months before, had fought their way through singing fire across these quiet fields, who had seen the men die who were buried here. There were troops who must soon go into battle again. There were everyday Americans gathering in their thousands. Above them all, on the open-air platform stood the leaders of the land. Their faces were turned towards the orator of the day, whose voice held the audience.

2   For two hours, Everett spoke and the throng listened. As had been expected, he spoke of the great battle, of the causes of the war, of the results to come. As the clear, cultivated voice fell silent, the mass of people burst into a long storm of applause, for they knew that they had heard an oration which was an event. They clapped and cheered him again and again. At last, the ex-Governor of Massachusetts, the ex-ambassador to England, the ex-Secretary of State, the ex-Senator of the United States took his seat.

3   Next, a tall, gaunt figure stood up, slouched slowly across the open space, and stood facing the audience. This was the President. His appearance was strange, disappointing. Then he spoke in a queer, squeaking voice. A titter ran through the crowd. After a pause almost too slight to be recognized, the President went on. In a dozen words, his tones had gathered volume. He had come to his power and dignity. That these were his people was his only thought. He had something to say to them; what did it matter about him or his voice?

4   "Fourscore and seven years ago," spoke the President, "our fathers brought forth upon this continent a new nation, conceived in liberty and dedicated to the proposition that all men are created equal. Now we are engaged in a great civil war, testing whether that nation, or any nation so conceived and so dedicated, can long endure. We are met on a great battlefield of that war. We have come to dedicate a portion of it as a final resting place for those who here gave their lives that that nation might live. It is altogether fitting and proper that we should do this.

5   "But in a larger sense we cannot dedicate, we cannot consecrate, we cannot hallow this ground. The brave men, living and dead, who struggled here have consecrated it far above our poor power to add or detract. The world will little note nor long remember what we say here, but it can never forget what they did here.

129

6   "It is for us, the living, rather, to be dedicated here to the unfinished work which they who fought here have thus far so nobly advanced. It is rather for us to be here dedicated to the great task remaining before us—that from these honored dead we take increased devotion to that cause for which they here gave the last full measure of devotion; that we here highly resolve that these dead shall not have died in vain; that this nation, under God, shall have a new birth of freedom; and that government of the people, by the people, for the people shall not perish from the earth."

7   When he finished speaking, there was no sound from the crowd. The President stood before them. He stared at them with sad eyes, and in the deep quiet they stared at him. Not a hand lifted in applause. Slowly the big, awkward man slouched back across the platform and sank into his seat. Still, there was no sound of approval, no recognition from the audience; only a long sigh ran through it like a ripple on an ocean. In Lincoln's heart, a throb of pain answered it. His speech had been—as he had feared it would be—a failure. As he gazed at his countrymen, who would not give him even a little perfunctory applause for his best effort, the disappointment cut into his soul. And then he was aware that there was music: the choir was singing a dirge. His part was done, and his part had failed.

8   When the ceremonies were over, Everett spoke to the President. "Mr. President," he began, "your speech ..." Lincoln interrupted with a smile, "We'll manage not to talk about my speech, Mr. Everett," he said. "This isn't the first time I've felt that my dignity ought not permit me to be a public speaker." He went on to compliment Everett on his oration.

9   Everett listened thoughtfully and, when the chief had done, said simply, "Mr. President, I should be glad if ... I came as near the central idea of the occasion in two hours as you did in two minutes."

1   Who was the first speaker?

     A   Lincoln
     B   Everett
     C   A soldier
     D   The Secretary of State

130

2   According to paragraph 1, when did the battle of Gettysburg happen?

   A   On November 19, 1863
   B   Four months before the ceremony
   C   Fourscore and seven years earlier
   D   The text does not give this information.

3   In paragraph 2, the word oration means —

   A   ceremony
   B   prayer
   C   speech
   D   tribute

4   In paragraph 3, why does the audience laugh at President Lincoln?

   A   They don't respect him.
   B   He makes a lot of jokes in his speech.
   C   His voice doesn't match his appearance.
   D   He has forgotten what he wanted to say.

5   The author tells this story so readers will understand that Lincoln —

   A   was a modest man
   B   had a high, squeaky voice
   C   was not good at public speaking
   D   was a very unpopular President

6   In this text, the author orders the events according to —

   A   cause and effect
   B   chronology
   C   comparison
   D   problem and solution

from THE SEEING HAND

by Helen Keller

1   I have just touched my dog. He was rolling on the grass with pleasure in every muscle and limb. I wanted to catch a picture of him in my fingers, and I touched him as lightly as I would cobwebs. But his fat body revolved, stiffened and solidified into an upright position, and his tongue gave my hand a lick! He pressed close to me, as if he were fain to crowd himself into my hand. He loved it with his tail, with his paw, with his tongue. If he could speak, I believe he would say with me that paradise is attained by touch, for in touch is all love and intelligence.

2   This small incident started me on a chat about hands… But at the very outset we encounter a difficulty. You are so accustomed to light, I fear you will stumble when I try to guide you through the land of darkness and silence. The blind are not supposed to be the best of guides. Still, . . . I promise that you shall not be led into fire or water, or fall into a deep pit. If you will follow me patiently, you will find that . . . there is more meant in things than meets the eye.

3   My hand is to me what your hearing and sight together are to you. In large measure, we travel the same highways, read the same books, speak the same language, yet our experiences are different. All my comings and goings turn on the hand as on a pivot. It is the hand that binds me to the world of men and women. The hand is my feeler, with which I reach through isolation and darkness and seize every pleasure, every activity that my fingers encounter. With the dropping of a little word from another's hand into mine—a slight <u>flutter</u> of the fingers—began the intelligence, the joy, the fullness of my life.

1   The author of this text is —

    A   blind
    B   afraid of dogs
    C   fond of long walks
    D   a very unhappy person

132

2   According to paragraph 1, both the writer and her dog —

    A   like to play
    B   rely on their hands
    C   love rolling in the grass
    D   know the importance of touch

3   According to paragraph 3, what is the main difference between the author and her readers?

    A   How she travels
    B   Which books she reads
    C   How she experiences the world
    D   What language she speaks

4   In paragraph 3, what does the word *flutter* mean?

    A   Bet
    B   Excitement
    C   Movement
    D   Wing

5   The last sentence of the text probably refers to —

    A   shaking hands
    B   sign language
    C   writing
    D   birds

from THE SECRET GARDEN
by Frances Hodgson Burnett

1   It was not until she climbed to the second floor that she thought of turning the handle of a door. All the doors were shut, as Mrs. Medlock had said they were, but at last she put her hand on the handle of one of them and turned it. She was almost frightened for a moment when she felt that it turned without difficulty and that when she pushed upon the door itself it slowly and heavily opened. It was a massive door and opened into a big bedroom. There were embroidered hangings on the wall, and inlaid furniture such as she had seen in India stood about the room. A broad window with leaded panes looked out upon the moor; and over the mantel was another portrait of the stiff, plain little girl who seemed to stare at her more curiously than ever.

2   "Perhaps she slept here once," said Mary. "She stares at me so that she makes me feel queer."

3   After that she opened more doors and more. She saw so many rooms that she became quite tired and began to think that there must be a hundred, though she had not counted them…

4   In all her wanderings through the long corridors and the empty rooms, she had seen nothing alive; but in this room she saw something. Just after she had closed the cabinet door she heard a tiny rustling sound. It made her jump and look around at the sofa by the fireplace, from which it seemed to come. In the corner of the sofa there was a cushion, and in the velvet which covered it there was a hole, and out of the hole peeped a tiny head with a pair of frightened eyes in it.

5   Mary crept softly across the room to look. The bright eyes belonged to a little gray mouse, and the mouse had eaten a hole into the cushion and made a comfortable nest there. Six baby mice were cuddled up asleep near her. If there was no one else alive in the hundred rooms there were seven mice who did not look lonely at all.

6   "If they wouldn't be so frightened I would take them back with me," said Mary.

7   She had wandered about long enough to feel too tired to wander any farther, and she turned back. Two or three times she lost her way by turning down the wrong corridor and was obliged to ramble up and down until she found the right one; but at last she reached her own floor again, though she was some distance from her own room and did not know exactly where she was.

134

8   "I believe I have taken a wrong turning again," she said, standing still at what seemed the end of a short passage with tapestry on the wall. "I don't know which way to go. How still everything is!"

9   It was while she was standing here and just after she had said this that the stillness was broken by a sound. It was another cry, but not quite like the one she had heard last night; it was only a short one, a fretful childish whine muffled by passing through walls.

10   "It's nearer than it was," said Mary, her heart beating rather faster. "And it is crying."

11   She put her hand accidentally upon the tapestry near her, and then sprang back, feeling quite startled. The tapestry was the covering of a door which fell open and showed her that there was another part of the corridor behind it, and Mrs. Medlock was coming up it with her bunch of keys in her hand and a very cross look on her face.

12   "What are you doing here?" she said, and she took Mary by the arm and pulled her away. "What did I tell you?"

13   "I turned round the wrong corner," explained Mary. "I didn't know which way to go and I heard someone crying." She quite hated Mrs. Medlock at the moment, but she hated her more the next.

14   "You didn't hear anything of the sort," said the housekeeper. "You come along back to your own nursery, or I'll box your ears."

15   And she took her by the arm and half pushed, half pulled her up one passage and down another until she pushed her in at the door of her own room.

1   The house where the story takes place is —

    A   very large
    B   abandoned
    C   full of mice
    D   where Mary grew up

2   Which of the following best describes Mary?

   A   Happy
   B   Lazy
   C   Lonely
   D   Naughty

3   In the passage, —

   A   Mary meets a strange girl
   B   Mary explores her new home
   C   Mary asks Mrs. Medlock for help
   D   Mrs. Medlock starts working as a housekeeper

4   Which of the following statements about Mrs. Medlock is true?

   A   She is hiding something.
   B   She probably smiles a lot.
   C   She makes Mary feel welcome.
   D   She doesn't believe in physical punishment.

136

from GREAT EXPECTATIONS, CHAPTER ONE
by Charles Dickens

1   "Hold your noise!" cried a terrible voice, as a man started up from among the graves at the side of the church porch. "Keep still, you little devil, or I'll cut your throat!"

2   A fearful man, all in coarse gray, with a great iron on his leg. A man with no hat, and with broken shoes, and with an old rag tied round his head. A man who had been soaked in water, and smothered in mud, and lamed by stones, and cut by flints, and stung by nettles, and torn by briars; who limped, and shivered, and glared, and growled; and whose teeth chattered in his head as he seized me by the chin.

3   "Oh! Don't cut my throat, sir," I pleaded in terror. "Pray don't do it, sir."

4   "Tell us your name!" said the man. "Quick!"

5   "Pip, sir."

6   "Once more," said the man, staring at me. "Give it mouth!"

7   "Pip. Pip, sir."

8   "Show us where you live," said the man. "Point out the place!" I pointed to where our village lay, on the flat in-shore among the alder-trees and pollards, a mile or more from the church.

9   The man, after looking at me for a moment, turned me upside down, and emptied my pockets. There was nothing in them but a piece of bread. When the church came to itself—for he was so sudden and strong that he made it go head over heels before me, and I saw the steeple under my feet—when the church came to itself, I say, I was seated on a high tombstone, trembling while he ate the bread ravenously.

10   "You young dog," said the man, licking his lips, "what fat cheeks you've got."

11   I believe they were fat, though I was at that time undersized for my years, and not strong.

12   "Darn me if I couldn't eat them," said the man, with a threatening shake of his head, "and if I hadn't half a mind to do it!"

13   I earnestly expressed my hope that he wouldn't, and held tighter to the tombstone on which he had put me—partly to keep myself upon it; partly to keep myself from crying.

14   "Now lookee here!" said the man. "Where's your mother?"

15   "There, sir!" said I. He started, made a short run, and stopped and looked over his shoulder. "There, sir!" I timidly explained. "'Also Georgiana'—that's my mother."

16   "Oh!" said he, coming back. "And is that your father alongside your mother?"

17   "Yes, sir," said I, "him too; 'late of this parish.'"

18   "Ha!" he muttered then, considering. "Who do you live with—supposing you're kindly let to live, which I haven't made up my mind about?"

19   "My sister, sir—Mrs. Joe Gargery—wife of Joe Gargery, the blacksmith, sir."

20   "Blacksmith, eh?" said he. And looked down at his leg. After darkly looking at his leg and me several times, he came closer to my tombstone, took me by both arms, and tilted me back as far as he could hold me; so that his eyes looked most powerfully down into mine, and mine looked most helplessly up into his. "Now lookee here," he said, "the question being whether you're to be let to live. You know what a file is?"

21   "Yes, sir."

22   "And you know what vittles is?"

23   "Yes, sir."

24   After each question he tilted me over a little more, so as to give me a greater sense of helplessness and danger.

25   "You get me a file." He tilted me again. "And you get me vittles." He tilted me again. "You bring them both to me." He tilted me again. "Or I'll have your heart and liver out." He tilted me again.

26   I was dreadfully frightened, and so giddy that I clung to him with both hands, and said, "If you would kindly please to let me keep upright, sir, perhaps I shouldn't be sick, and perhaps I could attend more."

27   He gave me a most tremendous dip and roll, so that the church jumped over its own weathercock. Then, he held me by the arms, in an upright position on

138

the top of the stone, and went on in these fearful terms: "You bring me, tomorrow morning early, that file and them vittles. You bring the lot to me, at that old battery over yonder. You do it, and you never dare to say a word or dare to make a sign concerning your having seen such a person as me, or any person whatsoever, and you shall be let to live. You fail, or you go from my words in any particular, no matter how small it is, and your heart and your liver shall be tore out, roasted, and ate. Now, I ain't alone, as you may think I am. There's a young man hid with me, in comparison with which young man I am an angel. That young man hears the words I speak. That young man has a secret way peculiar to himself, of getting at a boy, and at his heart, and at his liver. It is in vain for a boy to attempt to hide himself from that young man. A boy may lock his door, may be warm in bed, may tuck himself up, may draw the clothes over his head, may think himself comfortable and safe, but that young man will softly creep and creep his way to him and tear him open. I am a keeping that young man from harming you at the present moment, with great difficulty. I find it very hard to hold that young man off of your inside. Now, what do you say?"

28   I said that I would get him the file, and I would get him what broken bits of food I could, and I would come to him at the battery, early in the morning.

29   "Say Lord strike you dead if you don't!" said the man. I said so, and he took me down. "Now," he pursued, "you remember what you've undertook, and you remember that young man, and you get home!"

30   "Goo-good night, sir," I faltered.

1   Where does Pip meet the man?

   A   At home
   B   At a church
   C   In a battery
   D   In a graveyard

2   The man is —

   A   with another, younger man
   B   cold, hungry, dirty, and injured
   C   probably the vicar of the nearby church
   D   a friend of Pip's sister and brother-in-law

3   Who is telling this story?

   A   Someone who knows the man
   B   Pip's sister
   C   The man
   D   Pip

4   In paragraphs 19 and 20, what does the man think when the boy says the word "blacksmith"?

   A   He hopes Pip comes from a rich family.
   B   He is afraid a strong blacksmith might hurt him.
   C   He thinks the blacksmith will have a tool to free him from his leg iron.
   D   He hopes Pip will take him home to sleep by the blacksmith's warm fire.

5   Why does the man keep talking about a "young man" who will eat Pip's heart and liver?

   A   To scare Pip into helping him
   B   To keep Pip from coming back the next day
   C   To explain why he is treating Pip so roughly
   D   To convince Pip to bring enough food for two

140

6   According to the text, where are Pip's parents?

A   at home
B   dead and buried
C   waiting for Pip nearby
D   visiting the blacksmith and his wife

7   What are vittles?

A   Tools
B   Drinks
C   Money
D   Food

7A   Which of the following passages supports the answer you provided to the question above?

A   "You get me a file." He tilted me again. "And you get me vittles." He tilted me again. "You bring them both to me." He tilted me again. "Or I'll have your heart and liver out." He tilted me again.

B   I was dreadfully frightened, and so giddy that I clung to him with both hands, and said, "If you would kindly please to let me keep upright, sir, perhaps I shouldn't be sick, and perhaps I could attend more."

C   I said that I would get him the file, and I would get him what broken bits of food I could, and I would come to him at the battery, early in the morning.

D   "Say Lord strike you dead if you don't!" said the man. I said so, and he took me down. "Now," he pursued, "you remember what you've undertook, and you remember that young man, and you get home!"

141

8 Do you think the setting makes this scene even more frightening? Why or why not?

_____

_____

_____

_____

_____

_____

_____

_____

_____

from GREAT EXPECTATIONS, CHAPTER TWO
by Charles Dickens

1   It was Christmas Eve, and I had to stir the pudding for next day with a copper-stick from seven to eight by the Dutch clock… "Hark!" said I, when I had done my stirring and was taking a final warm in the chimney corner before being sent up to bed, "was that great guns, Joe?"

2   "Ah!" said Joe. "There's another convict off."

3   "What does that mean, Joe?" said I.

4   Mrs. Joe, who always took explanations upon herself, said snappishly, "Escaped. Escaped." Administering the definition like Tar-water.

5   While Mrs. Joe sat with her head bending over her needlework, I put my mouth into the forms of saying to Joe, "What's a convict?" Joe put his mouth into the forms of returning such a highly elaborate answer, that I could make out nothing of it but the single word "Pip."

6   "There was a convict off last night," said Joe, aloud, "after sunset-gun. And they fired warning of him. And now it appears they're firing warning of another."

7   "Who's firing?" said I.

8   "Drat that boy," interposed my sister, frowning at me over her work, "what a questioner he is! Ask no questions, and you'll be told no lies."

9   It was not very polite to herself, I thought, to imply that I should be told lies by her even if I did ask questions. But she never was polite unless there was company.

10   At this point, Joe greatly augmented my curiosity by taking the utmost pains to open his mouth very wide, and to put it into the form of a word that looked to me like "sulks."

11   Therefore, I naturally pointed to Mrs. Joe, and put my mouth into the form of saying, "Her?"

12   But Joe wouldn't hear of that at all, and again opened his mouth very wide and shook the form of a most emphatic word out of it. But I could make nothing of the word.

13 "Mrs. Joe," said I, as a last resort, "I should like to know—if you wouldn't much mind—where the firing comes from?"

14 "Lord bless the boy!" exclaimed my sister, as if she didn't quite mean that but rather the contrary. "From the Hulks!"

15 "Oh-h!" said I, looking at Joe. "Hulks!"

16 Joe gave a reproachful cough, as much as to say, "Well, I told you so."

17 "And please, what's Hulks?" said I.

18 "That's the way with this boy!" exclaimed my sister, pointing me out with her needle and thread and shaking her head at me. "Answer him one question, and he'll ask you a dozen directly. Hulks are prison-ships, right across the meshes." We always used that name for marshes in our country.

19 "I wonder who's put into prison-ships, and why they're put there?" said I, in a general way, and with quiet desperation.

20 It was too much for Mrs. Joe, who immediately rose. "I tell you what, young fellow," said she, "I didn't bring you up by hand to badger people's lives out. It would be blame to me and not praise if I had. People are put in the Hulks because they murder and because they rob and forge and do all sorts of bad, and they always begin by asking questions. Now, you get along to bed!"

21 I was never allowed a candle to light me to bed, and, as I went upstairs in the dark, with my head tingling—from Mrs. Joe's thimble having played the tambourine upon it to accompany her last words—I felt fearfully sensible of the great convenience that the Hulks were handy for me. I was clearly on my way there. I had begun by asking questions, and I was going to rob Mrs. Joe.

22 Since that time, which is far enough away now, I have often thought that few people know what secrecy there is in the young under terror. No matter how unreasonable the terror, so that it be terror. I was in mortal terror of the young man who wanted my heart and liver; I was in mortal terror of my interlocutor with the iron leg; I was in mortal terror of myself, from whom an awful promise had been extracted; I had no hope of deliverance through my all-powerful sister, who repulsed me at every turn; I am afraid to think of what I might have done on requirement, in the secrecy of my terror.

1   Who is Mrs. Joe?

    A   A visitor
    B   Pip's sister
    C   The blacksmith
    D   A stranger Pip has robbed

2   In this chapter, what does Pip learn about the man he met in the graveyard?

    A   Joe knows who the man is.
    B   The man is an escaped convict.
    C   The man used to ask a lot of questions.
    D   The man is probably trying to get home to the ships.

3   Who does Pip feel he can trust the most?

    A   Joe
    B   Pip's sister
    C   The man in the graveyard
    D   The young man who wants his heart and liver

4   In the course of this conversation, Mrs. Joe —

    A   is very patient
    B   seems to be very lazy
    C   convinces Pip that he will end up going to prison
    D   keeps Pip safe and secure because she is all-powerful

5 Pip cannot ask Joe for help because

   A Joe is dangerous
   B Pip's sister holds all the power
   C Joe never listens to what Pip tells him
   D Pip does not want to get Joe into trouble

6 In the last paragraph, what is Pip saying?

   A Children are often afraid.
   B Having to keep secrets is scary.
   C Some dangers are real, and some are not.
   D Great fear makes children feel alone and desperate.

7 What does Pip's sister tell him will start someone on a life of crime?

   A Lying
   B Cheating
   C Asking questions
   D Laziness

7A Which of the following passages supports the answer you provided to the question above?

A "That's the way with this boy!" exclaimed my sister, pointing me out with her needle and thread and shaking her head at me. "Answer him one question, and he'll ask you a dozen directly. Hulks are prison-ships, right across the meshes." We always used that name for marshes in our country.

B It was too much for Mrs. Joe, who immediately rose. "I tell you what, young fellow," said she, "I didn't bring you up by hand to badger people's lives out. It would be blame to me and not praise if I had. People are put in the Hulks because they murder and because they rob and forge and do all sorts of bad, and they always begin by asking questions. Now, you get along to bed!"

C I was never allowed a candle to light me to bed, and, as I went upstairs in the dark, with my head tingling—from Mrs. Joe's thimble having played the tambourine upon it to accompany her last words—I felt fearfully sensible of the great convenience that the Hulks were handy for me. I was clearly on my way there. I had begun by asking questions, and I was going to rob Mrs. Joe.

D "I wonder who's put into prison-ships, and why they're put there?" said I, in a general way, and with quiet desperation.

8 Do you think the time of year is important to this story?

Answers will vary, but many should point out that the fact that it is

Christmas Eve makes Pip's sad life seem even worse at a time that should be

full of happiness.

_____

_____

_____

_____

THE LOST CITY OF ATLANTIS

1   We all lose things from time to time. Sometimes you'll lose a favorite book or a letter you wrote to a friend. Some things simply seem to vanish into thin air, like all of those socks that disappear in the wash. Small objects are easily lost, but could you imagine losing something as large as a city? That's just what happened to the city of Atlantis thousands of years ago. Over the years, some people have searched for the lost island city while others have questioned whether it was real in the first place.

2   Thousands of years ago, a writer and philosopher named Plato lived in Greece. Plato was a very wise man who studied history and math. In his books, Plato would try to make a point by using different characters. These characters would often argue over an idea. Plato used these stories to help people understand his ideas about things. Some of his characters were real people and others were completely made up.

3   One of Plato's characters told the story of Atlantis. The character explained that Atlantis was on an island in the Atlantic Ocean. The island was described as an almost magical place, built by the sea god Poseidon. The story said that the people of the island would live happy lives as long as they followed the god's rules.

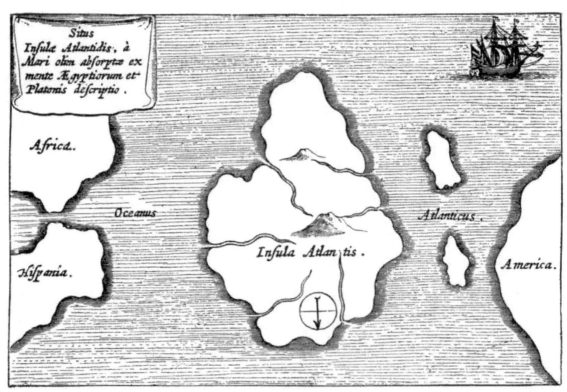

Legendary island of Atlantis described by Plato and said to lie just beyond the Pillars of Hercules (Gibraltar and Mount Hacho). Engraving based on description by Athanasius Kircher (1602-1680), German Jesuit priest and scientist.

148

4   For many years, few problems troubled Atlantis. The people of the island built amazing buildings and tunnels. The people grew all of the food that they needed in carefully planted fields. Based on the story, these people were ahead of the rest of the world by leaps and bounds. They knew how to keep a house warm in the winter and cool in the summer. They did this without having any of the machines we use today. Atlantis soon became a very important city.

5   After a while, the island's leaders became greedy. They loved power more than they loved the gods. The people soon turned their backs on the rules that Poseidon had made. This made the gods very angry. The Atlantians fought against many other great countries. Though they were strong, the people of Atlantis lost. After this, the gods stopped protecting the island and let it sink into the sea.

The philosopher Plato introduced the city of Atlantis to the Greek people.

6   Many people believed that Plato used the story of Atlantis to make a point. The story was meant to show people why they shouldn't be greedy. Most people thought that Plato had made Atlantis up. Besides, no one else had ever written about the island before.

7   Though few believed in the lost city, the story continued to interest people for hundreds of years. More books were written about Atlantis. Most were just for fun, but some writers believed that Atlantis had been real.

8   Ignatius Donnelly believed in Atlantis. The American writer said he had discovered the spot where the island had been. He wrote a book about his ideas and sold many copies. At this time, there was no way to tell if Donnelly was right. Years later, a team went down to bottom of the Atlantic Ocean. They couldn't find any sign of Atlantis.

9   People still believed in Atlantis. They just thought the island must be in another place. The search for Atlantis spread all over the world. Some people think the lost city is near Florida and others think it might be closer to Australia.

10   If Atlantis was real, scientists seem sure that a natural event probably caused the island to sink. This idea might also help them find the island. History books tell us that a volcano blew up on an island in the Mediterranean Sea many years ago. A group of people known as the Minoans lived on a nearby island. Like the people of Atlantis, the Minoans had had a beautiful city and had lived happily. The Minoans also seemed to disappear in the blink of an eye. Scientists believe the volcano made a very large wave that hit the Minoans' island and wrecked their city.

11

Archaeologists carefully study Minoan ruins by constructing covered areas like these. In this photograph, you can clearly see that at least one building has been uncovered.

Some people think that the Minoans' island was the real Atlantis, while others say that this data doesn't match Plato's story. We may never know if the city was real or where it once stood. Until we find an answer, people will probably continue searching for Atlantis for many years to come.

1   If Atlantis was real, it most likely sank into the ocean because

A   a huge wave hit the island.
B   the gods stopped guarding it.
C   a volcano wrecked the city.
D   the people left the island.

150

2 Why do many people think that Atlantis was not a real place? Use information
   from the article to support your response.

_____

_____

_____

_____

_____

_____

_____

_____

_____

_____

_____

_____

_____

_____

_____

_____

_____

3　Why do you think the author started this article by writing the first paragraph the way he or she did? Do you think that the first paragraph fits this article? If yes, explain why. If no, explain how you would change the first paragraph. Use information from the article to support your response.

_____

_____

_____

_____

_____

_____

_____

_____

_____

_____

_____

_____

_____

_____

_____

_____

_____

4   Do you think that Atlantis was real?

- If so, what do you think probably happened to the city?
- If not, why do you think people probably still look for the city?

Use information from the article to support your response.

_____

_____

_____

_____

_____

_____

_____

_____

_____

_____

_____

_____

_____

_____

JEFFREY'S NEW BEGINNING

1   Jeffrey and Stacy were sitting on Stacy's porch when they decided to do one of their favorite things. They gathered the loose change they had in their pockets and walked to the corner store. Stacy and Jeffrey loved nothing more than buying the newspaper and hanging out on the porch trading sections with each other as they finished reading them over a long afternoon. After six years of being best friends, they had shared many newspapers together.

2   When Jeffrey went home that hot summer night after a fun day of reading and playing with Stacy, he could tell that something was wrong. As he walked into the living room, he noticed boxes and newspaper lying all over the floor. His mother and father must have heard the door close because they walked into the room to greet him.

4   "Hey, Jeff! There's something we need to talk to you about," said Mrs. Anderson. She bent down so that she could look into Jeffrey's eyes as she gave him the news.

5   "You're father was just offered a great job and has decided to take it," she said.

154

6   "The only thing, Jeff," said Mr. Anderson, "is that we have to move to Chicago in a few days because they want me to start right away. We have to hurry, and we're going to need your help. Okay, Big Guy?" Mr. Anderson patted Jeffrey's head.

7   Jeffrey was not happy. He ran past his parents, flew up the steps and into his bedroom, and closed the door behind him.

8   Jeffrey thought about why he suddenly felt so sad. After a few minutes, he realized that he didn't want to leave Springfield, and he really didn't want to leave Stacy. He felt like he had to do something!

8   He waited until 9:00 P.M. when he knew that his parents would be downstairs on the couch watching TV. Then, Jeffrey walked down the stairs and stood right in front of the TV to block their view. He wanted their complete attention.

9   "I have made up my mind. I do not want to go to Chicago," said Jeffrey.

10   Jeffrey's parents knew how important his and Stacy's friendship was and did feel very bad about Jeffrey's having to move away from her and Springfield.

11   "Jeffrey," said Mrs. Anderson, "your father and I have already talked to Stacy's parents. On some weekends, we can drive you here, and on some weekends, they can bring Stacy to our new place. We are only going to be two hours away. It's not the end of the world, honey. Think of it as a new beginning . . . for all of us."

12   "And Jeff, think about all the fun that we're going to have in the big city," said Mr. Anderson. "I was going to wait until we got there to tell you this, but I bought tickets for us to go to Wrigley Field to see a baseball game next weekend, and Stacy's parents said that she could come with us!"

13   Jeffrey smiled from ear to ear even though he was still a little upset. Stacy and he loved baseball, and he couldn't wait to tell her about the game!

14   He gave his parents each a hug, ran to the living room to grab some boxes, and then went upstairs to start packing his room. He was suddenly so excited about the move that he spent all day Wednesday packing and asking questions about Chicago.

15   When the day before moving day rolled around, the Andersons (especially Jeffrey) were all very tired. Jeffrey had just finished packing the last of his things   when

he heard the doorbell ring. He ran to open the door and saw that it was Stacy. Jeffrey could tell that she had been crying and figured that her parents had told her the news.

16   "I just wanted to tell you that I hope you have lots of fun in Chicago and that I will miss you very much," Stacy said. She gave Jeffrey a quick hug and turned to run back down the steps.

17   "Stacy, wait," called Jeffrey. "Please come back."

18   Stacy stopped and turned around. Jeffrey sat down on the top step and motioned for Stacy to come and sit next to him.

19   "It's not going to be so bad, Stacy. We won't be right down the street from each other, and we won't go to the same school anymore, but I will only be a few hours away. We will still get to play together on the weekends, and we will always be best friends. Just think of all the neat stuff we will get to do in the big city—parks with lots of rides, museums, and best of all, we get to go to see a baseball game next weekend with my dad. Maybe afterwards we can buy the big, thick Chicago paper and hang out on my new porch together."

20   Stacy's eyes gleamed with excitement as Jeffrey described all the places they were going to go and things they were going to see. She was happy Jeffrey hadn't forgotten about her. She and Jeffrey were going to have so much fun!

21 After a few minutes, Stacy was okay with the whole idea and, even though she knew she was going to miss having him so close, she could not wait to spend time with Jeffrey in Chicago. The museums and baseball games seemed very exciting! Plus, she was happy Jeffrey liked their lazy newspaper afternoons as much as she did.

22 "Do you need any help getting packed?" asked Stacy.

23 Jeffrey smiled. "I have a better idea. Come on, let's go!"

24 Jeffrey and Stacy played all day in the tree house and imagined and planned what they would do when they saw each other throughout the rest of the summer.

25 The next morning, Jeffrey and Stacy helped his parents load the moving truck. When it was time to go, they waved goodbye, knowing that they would see each other soon and have lots of fun. Even though saying goodbye was sad, Jeffrey and Stacy were excited about their new beginnings.

1   How do you think that Stacy was feeling when she came to tell Jeffrey that she would miss him when he moved to Chicago? Use information from the story to support your response.

_____

_____

_____

_____

_____

_____

_____

_____

_____

_____

_____

_____

_____

_____

_____

_____

_____

2 What do you think will happen to Jeffrey and Stacy over the next summer? Use information from the story to support your response.

_____

_____

_____

_____

_____

_____

_____

_____

_____

_____

_____

_____

_____

_____

_____

_____

_____

_____

3   Based on what you've read in the story, what do you think the town where Jeffrey and Stacy live is like? How do you think it is different from Chicago? Use information from the story to support your response.

_____

_____

_____

_____

_____

_____

_____

_____

_____

_____

_____

_____

_____

_____

_____

_____

_____

4 Do you think that Jeffrey's parents could have done anything to make moving easier for him, or do you think they did everything that they could do? Use information from the story to support your response.

_____

_____

_____

_____

_____

_____

_____

_____

_____

_____

_____

_____

_____

_____

_____

_____

A VERY FANCY FROG

1   Amphibians (am-FIB-ee-enz) are a lot different than you are. They are cold-blooded, which means their bodies stay hot from the sun. They breathe air through their skin, instead of through their mouths and noses like you do. They live both in water and on land.

2   Frogs are a kind of amphibian. There are many different kinds of frogs. One kind of frog is a red-eyed tree frog. Red-eyed tree frogs are tiny, bright green frogs with huge, red eyes. They sometimes have colorful stripes, lines, and spots on their backs and legs. The stripes can be blue, yellow, red, and pink. At the end of each foot are orange toes.

3   Red-eyed tree frogs are really pretty! Their pretty colors help keep them safe from bigger animals that might eat them. The colors are called "flash colors" because they flash in the bigger animals' eyes. The animals don't know where to find the frogs.

4   Red-eyed tree frogs live in rainforests. The rainforest is much different from where you live. It is hot all year in the rainforest and it rains a lot, which is how it got its name. Red-eyed tree frogs need to keep their skin wet all the time so they can breathe air. The rain in the rainforest helps them to be able to do this.

5   Red-eyed tree frogs like to sleep on leaves, sometimes in little piles of frogs. They like to live in groups with other red-eyed tree frogs. Red-eyed tree frogs sleep during the day, and they are awake at night. Their big red eyes help them see when it is dark outside. At night, they look for food to eat. Red-eyed tree frogs mostly eat insects. Sometimes, they even eat smaller frogs!

6   Red-eyed tree frogs can be pretty noisy. Sometimes, they make a little ticking noise, almost like a clock makes. Other times, they sound more like a bird or a monkey.

162

7   Red-eyed tree frogs are sometimes called "monkey frogs." They can hop like most other frogs do. But they can walk by moving their front legs and back legs at the same time. In fact, red-eyed tree frogs are the only frogs that walk this way. These frogs can jump really far, too. They like to climb a lot. The bottoms of their feet are sticky, which helps them climb.

8   Red-eyed tree frogs lay eggs to have babies. They lay these eggs on leaves in trees. When the baby frogs are ready to be born, they move around the eggs until they fall into a pond that is under the leaf, which is where they are born. Baby red-eyed tree frogs look a little like fish. But when they grow up, they are just as pretty as their parents!

1   Why are red-toed tree frogs sometimes called "monkey frogs?"

A   they can jump real far
B   the bottoms of their feet are sticky
C   they move their front legs and back legs at the same time when walking
D   they have orange toes

1A   Which of the following passages supports the answer you provided to the question above?

    A   Red-eyed tree frogs lay eggs to have babies. They lay these eggs on leaves in trees. When the baby frogs are ready to be born, they move around the eggs until they fall into a pond that is under the leaf, which is where they are born.

    B   Red-eyed tree frogs are sometimes called "monkey frogs." They can hop like most other frogs do. But they can walk by moving their front legs and back legs at the same time. In fact, red-eyed tree frogs are the only frogs that walk this way.

    C   They like to climb a lot. The bottoms of their feet are sticky, which helps them climb.

    D   Red-eyed tree frogs are tiny, bright green frogs with huge, red eyes. They sometimes have colorful stripes, lines, and spots on their backs and legs. The stripes can be blue, yellow, red, and pink. At the end of each foot are orange toes.

2   Would you like to see a red-eyed tree frog in a zoo or pet store? Use
    information from the article to support your answer.

_____

_____

_____

_____

_____

_____

_____

_____

_____

_____

_____

_____

_____

_____

_____

_____

_____

_____

165

THE MYSTERY AT THE CABIN

1   Hilary leaned her head against the car window. She gazed at the red, yellow, orange, and brown leaves that lined the road. They were getting close to the cabin, and she couldn't wait until they arrived.

2   The cabin was made of logs and sat in the woods near a lake. Her grandfather had built it a long time ago. It was not a fancy place. It had running water and lights, but that was about it. The water never got hot. When it rained, water leaked through the roof in a few spots.

3   Even so, Hilary loved it there, especially when her family met up with her cousin's family for a long weekend. Some of Hilary's favorite memories took place during those times. Her dad would build roaring fires in the fireplace. She and her cousin, Christina, would sit in front of the fire and play board games for hours. They would drink hot chocolate and warm apple cider. They would make up stories to scare each other. Then, they would make up funny stories to make each other forget the scary ones.

4   As Hilary's father stopped the car in front of the cabin, Hilary saw Christina waiting on the porch. She jumped out of the car and gave her cousin a big hug.

5   "I missed you, Christina!" Hilary exclaimed.

6   "I missed you, too," said Christina.

7   After Hilary had hugged her Aunt Mary and Uncle Joe, she and Christina quickly carried blankets and bags into the cabin. They talked the whole time, telling each other about their schools, their teachers, and their friends. That night, their parents made a big dinner. They had hamburgers, baked potatoes, and corn on the cob. When they had finished eating, Aunt Mary asked Hilary and Christina to clean the table. The two girls put all the dishes in the sink.

166

They took all the corncobs and potato skins outside and put them in the garbage can. Hilary pressed on the lid to make sure that it was closed. Then, the two girls went inside to play a game.

8   The next morning, Hilary and Christina were surprised to find their parents in the kitchen with frowns on their faces.

9   "Girls, we told you to put the food scraps in the garbage last night," said Hilary's mother.

10   "Take a look out the window," said Aunt Mary.

11   Hilary and Christina glanced out the window. The lid was off the garbage can. Corncobs and potato skins lay all over the little porch.

12   "We didn't do that," said Christina. "The lid was on tight last night."

13   Aunt Mary raised her eyebrows. "Did someone just walk by, open the garbage can, and throw food all over the porch?"

14   "I don't know," said Christina, "but I know that we didn't make that mess."

15   The girls had no idea how the food had ended up on the porch, but they cleaned up the mess anyway. As they worked, they tried to figure out what happened.

16   "Maybe the wind blew the lid off," said Christina.

17   "Maybe," said Hilary. "But how did all the food scraps get out of the garbage can? They didn't jump out." Hilary thought for a moment as she dumped a handful of corncobs into the garbage can. "This is a mystery. Tonight, we should pretend to be police officers and watch to see if this happens again."

18   "That's a good idea," said Christina.

19 That night, Uncle Joe cooked fish and mixed vegetables for dinner. When dinner was over, the girls emptied the plates into the garbage can. Once again, Hilary tightly closed the lid. She followed Christina into the house, and they sat by the fire reading books.

20 After everyone had gone to bed, Hilary and Christina snuck back into the kitchen. They set a bench beneath the kitchen window and sat on it. The moon shined like a giant flashlight. They could see everything on the porch outside. They waited a long time. Their eyes began to get sleepy. Suddenly, they heard a noise and their eyes snapped wide open.

21 SCRITCH. SCRATCH. SCRITCH. SCRATCH.

22 The two girls pressed their noses to the window.

23 "What is that?" whispered Christina.

24 Hilary held a finger to her lips and pointed to the bottom step of the porch. The eyes of a small animal glowed back at them. The animal looked around as if it knew that it was getting into mischief, and then it ran up the steps. As it stepped into the moonlight, Hilary saw that their mysterious visitor was a raccoon. The black mask around its eyes made it look like a thief trying to  hide its face. Soon, two more raccoons joined the first one on the porch. Hilary and Christina watched as the raccoons worked together to remove the lid from the garbage can. Their paws moved like little hands. Once the lid was off, each raccoon grabbed some food scraps and ate a feast on the porch.

25 "What should we do?" asked Christina.

26 "I think we should wake up our parents so they know that it wasn't us who made that mess," said Hilary.

27 Christina agreed, and the two girls tiptoed to their parents' bedrooms and woke them up.

168

28   "What's wrong?" they asked, almost at the same time.

29   "Nothing," the girls said.

30   "Just follow us and stay quiet," said Hilary.

31   The girls led their parents into the kitchen and pointed toward the window. They gazed for a few minutes at the raccoons, watching them munch on leftover fish and vegetables. Then, they turned to the girls.

32   "We're sorry," said Hilary's father. "You had nothing to do with that mess this morning and we made you clean it up anyway."

33   "It's all right," said Hilary. "We didn't mind cleaning up the mess. We just wanted you to know that we were telling the truth."

34   "Well, we believe you now," said Aunt Mary. She kissed each of the girls on the head.

35   By that time, it was very late and the girls' parents sent them to bed. As Hilary pulled the blankets close to her chin, she thought about watching the little bandits on the porch. She was sure that she would remember them for a long time to come.

1   What time of year is it when this story takes place?

    A   summer
    B   fall
    C   winter
    D   spring

1A   Which of the following passages supports the answer you provided to the question above?

  A   Some of Hilary's favorite memories took place during those times. Her dad would build roaring fires in the fireplace.
  B   Hilary and Christina glanced out the window. The lid was off the garbage can. Corncobs and potato skins lay all over the little porch.
  C   As Hilary pulled the blankets close to her chin, she thought about watching the little bandits on the porch. She was sure that she would remember them for a long time to come.
  D   Hilary leaned her head against the car window. She gazed at the red, yellow, orange, and brown leaves that lined the road.

2   What is the log cabin missing?

  A   lights
  B   electricity
  C   plumbing
  D   a hot water heater

2A   Which of the following passages supports the answer you provided to the question above?

   A   The cabin was made of logs and sat in the woods near a lake. Her grandfather had built it a long time ago. It was not a fancy place. It had running water and lights, but that was about it. The water never got hot. When it rained, water leaked through the roof in a few spots.

   B   That night, Uncle Joe cooked fish and mixed vegetables for dinner. When dinner was over, the girls emptied the plates into the garbage can.

   C   That night, their parents made a big dinner. They had hamburgers, baked potatoes, and corn on the cob. When they had finished eating, Aunt Mary asked Hilary and Christina to clean the table. The two girls put all the dishes in the sink. They took all the corncobs and potato skins outside and put them in the garbage can.

   D   Some of Hilary's favorite memories took place during those times. Her dad would build roaring fires in the fireplace. She and her cousin, Christina, would sit in front of the fire and play board games for hours. They would drink hot chocolate and warm apple cider.

3 Do you think the events in the story "The Mystery at the Cabin" could really happen? Why or why not? Use information from the story to support your answer. Write your answer on the lines below.

_____

_____

_____

_____

_____

_____

_____

_____

_____

_____

_____

_____

_____

_____

_____

_____

_____

_____

SHARI HAD A LITTLE LAMB
by Barry Sterling

1   Shari Lewis loved making people laugh. When Shari was a little girl, she discovered that she could throw her voice. This meant that she could make it sound like her voice was coming from someplace else. Once, she used this skill to make her dad think that a voice was coming from the closet. When he opened the door, he saw that the closet was empty. After her dad realized that it had been Shari's voice coming from the closet, he knew that his daughter had a special skill!

"The Shari Lewis Show," 1960

2   Her dad worked as a teacher, but he also performed in magic shows. Shari's father showed his daughter how to do many magic tricks. At thirteen, Shari started helping her dad during these shows. The young girl shined whenever she was on the stage. Shari also inherited her love of music from her mother, who was a piano teacher. Shari took music lessons in high school where she learned to act and dance.

3   Though Shari had many skills, her real gift was working with puppets. Shari could make her puppets talk without moving her lips. She designed her own characters and gave them all different voices. Both grownups and children enjoyed watching her puppet shows. Shari decided to enter a television talent contest. Though there were many amazing acts, Shari and her puppets won first place. This was the start of something big!

4   A year later, Shari and one of her puppets appeared on the morning television show "Captain Kangaroo." The puppet was made from a fuzzy white sock and looked like a little a lamb. The puppet's name was Lamb Chop. Shari threw her voice to make Lamb Chop talk. Shari's great skills made it difficult for people to tell that she was speaking for Lamb Chop. People thought Lamb Chop and Shari made quite a funny pair. During the show, they made jokes, sang songs, and told stories. Shari and Lamb Chop were so popular that they were offered their own show the following year.

5   Shari and Lamb Chop were the stars, but many other puppets joined them on their morning show. Shari made a new group of friends to join Lamb Chop on their adventures. Characters like Hush Puppy and Charlie Horse joined Lamb Chop and Shari on the show every day. "The Shari Lewis Show" taught kids lessons while amusing them with songs, games, and riddles. Lamb Chop and her fellow puppets became friends to thousands of children across the country.

6   After the show ended, Shari continued working with her puppets. For a few years, she worked on a television show in England. Shari also began writing books for children. In her life, she completed over 60 books! During her time away from television, Shari traveled around the world as a music conductor.

7   Shari returned to television years later with Lamb Chop at her side to host "Lamb Chop's Play-Along." Though many kids were now watching cartoons, Shari believed that her puppets could still interest them. This new show introduced Lamb Chop and her pals to the children and grandchildren of the kids Shari had entertained many years before. Again, parents and children around the country loved the puppets. Besides working on her show, Shari also recorded songs and made a number of television specials.

8   Though Shari wanted kids to enjoy watching her show, she wanted to make sure that her program gave them useful information, too. The show allowed children to play games and sing songs while they learned important lessons. Shari was very interested in helping children learn. For many years, she worked with groups like the Boy and Girl Scouts of America. Shari also gave her time to programs that helped children learn to read. She was honored for all of her hard work with many different awards.

9   Shari and Lamb Chop put on shows for many famous people over the years. Though they performed for American presidents and the queen of England, what Shari loved most was making kids smile. Shari was certainly one of the best television performers of all time.

10 Today, Shari's daughter Mallory continues to put on shows with Lamb Chop. The two have traveled all over the world, performing for everyone from soldiers to school kids.

1   Who was the most famous puppet?

   A   Hush Puppy
   B   Charlie Horse
   C   Lamb Chop
   D   Captain Kangaroo

1A   Which of the following passages supports the answer you provided to the question above?

   A   Shari and Lamb Chop were the stars, but many other puppets joined them on their morning show.
   B   Shari made a new group of friends to join Lamb Chop on their adventures. Characters like Hush Puppy and Charlie Horse joined Lamb Chop and Shari on the show every day.
   C   "The Shari Lewis Show" taught kids lessons while amusing them with songs, games, and riddles. Lamb Chop and her fellow puppets became friends to thousands of children across the country.
   D   A year later, Shari and one of her puppets appeared on the morning television show "Captain Kangaroo." The puppet was made from a fuzzy white sock and looked like a little a lamb. The puppet's name was Lamb Chop. Shari threw her voice to make Lamb Chop talk. Shari's great skills made it difficult for people to tell that she was speaking for Lamb Chop.

175

2　The article says that Shari's real skill was working with puppets. Do you agree that that was her real skill?

_____

_____

_____

_____

_____

_____

_____

_____

_____

_____

_____

_____

_____

_____

_____

_____

_____

　176

PRACTICING BASEBALL

1   On the first day of summer break, my dad took me outside to work on my pitching. He said that this would be our summertime custom. We would practice every day. By the time I went back to school, he had explained, I should be playing like someone headed for the big leagues.

2   Practice was really fun—for about two weeks. On the last Saturday in June, I had to drag myself out of bed in order to get dressed, gather my ball and glove, and head down to the pitching spot Dad had worn into the grass in our backyard. Mom watched proudly from the window as Dad called out a pitch.

3   "Send me a curve ball, Mario!"

4   I lobbed him a curve ball that landed in the center of his glove.

5   "Headed for the big leagues," he called out.

6   I had imagined myself growing up to be a big league pitcher ever since Dad had taken me to a big league baseball game when I was little. We sat in the stands and searched our team yearbooks for each player who was batting. Dad would tell me stuff about the player while I watched every move the pitcher made. Now, however, I wondered how I'd ever be a big league player when after two weeks of practice, I was sick and tired of the game.

7   On the following Tuesday, Dad woke me by saying, "Let's play ball!"

8   I turned over in bed and muttered into my pillow, "I don't want to be a big league baseball player." It was good to say it out loud. It made me feel better, even if I was the only one who could hear it—or so I thought.

177

9 "What was that?" asked my dad. He had been right outside my room and had heard me. I was worried about what he would think. Even though I had learned that I didn't like playing baseball as much as I thought, I knew he dreamed of me becoming a pitcher one day. We looked at each other for a few seconds. Then Dad asked, "Are you telling me you don't want to practice anymore?"

10 That's not what I was saying at all. I explained that I did want to keep practicing. I wanted to be great. I just knew I didn't want to play baseball every day of my life. Some days, I wanted to go swimming or hang out with my friends. Other days I just wanted to lie in the grass read a book.

11 To my surprise, Dad said he knew how I felt. He said he was sorry and explained that all that talking we did about different baseball players made him happy and excited. He said he missed those old times when we used to go to games together. I missed those times too. So, after our talk, we put away the ball and glove and headed to the sports field in town. Only, we didn't head to the pitcher's mound. Instead, my dad and I enjoyed a game from the stands—just like old times.

1   What day is skipped over in this story?

   A   Sunday
   B   Monday
   C   Tuesday
   D   Wednesday

1A   Which of the following passages supports the answer you provided to the
     question above?

   A   On the first day of summer break, my dad took me outside to work on my
       pitching. He said that this would be our summertime custom. We would
       practice every day. By
   B   On the last Saturday in June, I had to drag myself out of bed in order to
       get dressed, gather my ball and glove, and head down to the pitching spot
       Dad had worn into the grass in our backyard
   C   On the following Tuesday, Dad woke me by saying, "Let's play ball!"
   D   I just knew I didn't want to play baseball every day of my life. Some days, I
       wanted to go swimming or hang out with my friends. Other days I just
       wanted to lie in the grass read a book.

2 Do you think Mario will become a big league pitcher one day? Use information from the story to support your response.

_____

_____

_____

_____

_____

_____

_____

_____

_____

_____

_____

_____

_____

_____

_____

_____

16 "Look at this!" yelled the spider. "I just wove this huge web in the time it took you to make one little, tiny thread of silk. Clearly, I'm the better weaver. I'll be the one the king favors!"

17 The silkworm did not yell back. Instead, he just kept quietly working. For more days, the silkworm made silk and then slowly began weaving it together. During this time, the spider lazily napped in his web, just waiting for the wedding day to arrive.

18 Finally, the important day arrived. Early that morning, both of the creatures raced to the king's chamber.

19 "King Bembledack!" called the spider. "I've made you a fine web robe that you can wear for your wedding."

20 "I have also made you a robe," said the silkworm.

21 "Fine! Thank you both," said King Bembledack, rising from his seat. "I was in need of a fine robe and I'm glad you took the time to provide one for me."

22 The silkworm and spider eagerly led King Bembledack toward their room. When he entered the room, the first thing he saw was a big, sticky spider's web. Before the spider could speak, the king said, "What a mess this room is!" He brushed at the web with his hands, knocking it down.

23 Once the web was gone, the king could see the robe the silkworm had made. It had wide sleeves, a beautiful color, and careful lacing around the neck.

24 "This is without a doubt the finest robe I have ever seen!" said King Bembledack. "I can tell that you spent many days carefully working on this."

25 The king picked up the robe and put it over his shoulders. It fit perfectly. He was so pleased with the robe that he said that the silkworm would be in charge of all his robes.

26   The spider, on the other hand, got no
      thanks at all. She was very angry when
      the king left. "I made that web so
      quickly—I think he should have been
      amazed by it!" she said.

27   "He saw that you didn't put much
      work into making that web," said
      the silkworm. "That's why he
      thought it was just an ugly mess
      and got rid of it. Making
      something really special
      takes a lot of work."

184

1 Why does the silkworm help the king? Use information from the story to support your response.

_____

_____

_____

_____

_____

_____

_____

_____

_____

_____

_____

185

21655519R00110

Made in the USA
Middletown, DE
10 July 2015